Books by John Fischer

FROM BETHANY HOUSE PUBLISHERS

Ashes on the Wind

On a Hill Too Far Away

Saint Ben

The Saints' and Angels' Song

True Believers ~~Don't~~ Ask Why

12 Steps for the Recovering Pharisee (like me)

JOHN FISCHER

ON a HILL
TOO
FAR AWAY

PUTTING *the* CROSS
BACK *into the*
CENTER *of* OUR LIVES

BETHANYHOUSE
MINNEAPOLIS, MINNESOTA

Published by Bethany House Publishers
A Ministry of Bethany Fellowship International
11400 Hampshire Avenue South
Bloomington, Minnesota 55438
www.bethanyhouse.com

Printed in the United States of America by
Bethany Press International, Bloomington, Minnesota 55438

Library of Congress Cataloging-in-Publication Data

Fischer, John, 1947–
    On a hill too far away : putting the cross back into the center of our
lives / by John Fischer.
       p. cm.
Originally published: Ann Arbor, Mich. : Vine Books, © 1994.
Includes bibliographical references.
    ISBN 0–7642–2470–0 (pbk.)
    1. Jesus Christ—Crucifixion. 2. Crosses. 3. Spiritual life—
Christianity. I. Title.
    BT453 .F49 2001
    232.96'3—dc21

                                                           00-011225

To the people of the
Presbyterian church of Old Greenwich, Connecticut,
and to its architect,
Rick Schoenhardt,
whose silent sermon preaches on.

JOHN FISCHER, pioneering musician, songwriter, and popular speaker, is also the award-winning author of many books. For years his insightful columns have been a favorite monthly feature in *Contemporary Christian Music Magazine*. A graduate of Wheaton College, John and his family live in California. For more information about John, visit his Web site at *www.fischtank.com*.

CONTENTS

INTRODUCTION

On a hill far away stood an old rugged cross,
The emblem of suff'ring and shame...

A THEOLOGY PROFESSOR at a Christian college recently told me that in America, by the last decade of the twentieth century, we had managed to recreate Christianity without a cross. Suddenly I understood what was wrong. The "me" decade of the '80s has rolled over into the church. Instead of coming before God in humility and fear, grateful for the breath to honor and serve him, we are more likely to come before him now to be blessed—to have our current desires bestowed upon us and to praise him on the basis of what we will receive in return.

This hasn't happened overnight, nor has it been intentional. Most likely this loss of the cross has grown out of a sincere evangelistic desire for the greatest possible number of people to become Christians. But too many adjustments have been made to this end, until the most important part of the gospel itself has been overlooked.

On a hill called Calvary, two thousand years ago, the Son of God was nailed to a cross for the real sins of the world. There was nothing pretty about the Crucifixion. When stripped of the religious sentiment of two thousand

9

years of symbolism and ornamentation, it appears as a gruesome and incomprehensible execution of God's most treasured human expression of himself.

Though historically central to the gospel and its daily presence in the life of a believer, the cross has faded away to the back wall of the church. There it stands as a suspended memory, lost in the more immediate attention given to the "felt needs" of people and the marketing of the new contemporary church. The hill was far away to begin with; now it is so far away that the old rugged cross tends to be forgotten in the current clamor for attention.

The purpose of this book is to bring the cross back to center stage in history and in the lives of Christians. Part 1 attempts to reestablish the incongruity of the gospel and the centrality of the cross to the Christian message. Part 2 deals with the role of the cross in the ongoing life of a believer. It shows how something as rugged and painful as the cross can actually become a cherished reality for those who meet their sin and salvation there on a daily basis.

Though the topic is theological in nature, this is not a theological book. It is a view from the trenches of contemporary Christianity by one who is struggling to understand what faith really means. The message of the cross seemed foolish when it was first proclaimed. If it has lost its foolishness, we must wonder if what we are hearing now is truly the same message the apostles had in mind: "For the time will come when men will not put up with sound doctrine. Instead, to suit their own desires, they will gather around them a great number of teachers to say what their itching ears want to hear" (2 Timothy 4:3).

This book is not comfortable reading for itching ears. It

is a book for those who want to get to the bottom of things—those who feel that something may be missing in the present-day proclamation of the Christian faith. It is for the spiritually young who are looking for substantial meat to cut their teeth on and for the older in faith who are longing for a good solid meal.

Thanks are in order to Ann Spangler for wrestling the topic from my writing, to Liz Heaney for helping me flesh it out, to Kathy Cunningham for checking my work along the way, to Nancy Nicholson for reading the manuscript, and to Steve Halliday for coming up with a title that says it all.

Additional thanks are in order with this edition to Randy Vader for turning this title into a musical and to Steve Laube and Bethany House Publishers for giving the book a second chance.

PART I

For Christ did not send me to baptize, but to preach the gospel—not with words of human wisdom, lest the cross of Christ be emptied of its power.

1 Corinthians 1:17

1

THE OLD GREENWICH
CROSS

IN OLD GREENWICH, CONNECTICUT, stands a church with a cross in it. Unlike most churches, whose crosses adorn the front wall behind the preacher, this one is bolted down into the concrete floor in front of the platform, not more than three feet from where the preacher stands.

Its positioning defies reason and art and convention. No architect in his right mind would have designed such a placement. It is an obstruction. The preacher's words have to pass through it; the congregation's eyes always have it somewhere in view, so that even when they look away, it is still there, impressed on the back wall of the retina.

It is a sturdy wooden cross, ten feet tall. The crossbar is set high on the vertical beam, so high that it seems out of proportion compared to other more proportionate crosses that decorate other more proportionate churches.

Nothing about this cross is pretty. It is made of raw, untreated wood, and when you see it up close, you think of splinters, of something hard . . . immovable. It is set deep in the concrete floor as well as bolted to it, so that a blow makes it vibrate rapidly. Strike it hard enough, and it will answer back in a low tone. I've heard that it can be removed, but not without great difficulty, because of its size and weight.

I got hit once with a baseball bat when I was a kid—walked right into my brother's backswing during a family softball game. The blow broke my nose. For some reason, that distant memory makes my face ache when I think about this cross—as if I might forget about it for a moment, turn around too quickly, and meet it head on.

But it would be almost impossible to forget about this cross. When I was standing and talking with someone or walking anywhere near the front of the church, I had a tendency to shy away from it—to lean unconsciously, to make sure I always knew where it was or, more accurately, where I was in relation to it.

The minute I walked into the church in Old Greenwich and encountered this startling placement of the cross, I felt as if I had discovered something truly significant. For just as the cross has been placed squarely in the center of this church, so it has always stood in the center of history and in the center of any life that has truly embraced it. And just as the placement of this cross seems uncomfortable, so it is . . . and so it should be. There is nothing comfortable about the cross.

This raw, wooden cross in the middle of the floor manages to defy the efforts we often make to soften its blow. Most crosses we encounter are harmless. They dangle from an ear or a wrist or lie in the nape of a pretty neck. They perch atop buildings or adorn the interior walls of our places of worship. The cross has become an ornament, a religious symbol mellowed by sentimental value. Some think that wearing a cross or hanging it on a wall makes God more favorably disposed to them. Others attribute some kind of magical or superstitious power to it, like a ballplayer signing the cross before he swings away.

The cross as a symbol has become more like a charm on a bracelet than a huge, rough, inconvenient reminder I might bump into in the front of a church. That is what makes this cross in Old Greenwich stand out. It is not something to wear or wish upon. You can't bring it into your life that easily. You can't hold it in your hand and bring it lovingly to your chest. You can't even pass your hand across its surface without getting splinters. The closest you could get to this cross would be to hug it, and hugging this cross is a little like hugging a tree.

The bold placement of this particular cross takes on a special significance in this dawning of a new millennium. The church in America has become increasingly accustomed to Christianity without a cross—or, at best, with one hanging harmlessly in the background. In our eagerness to popularize Christianity, we have created a very user-friendly gospel that asks for hardly a sacrifice. We have forgotten that in the middle of this gospel stands a cross—an instrument of execution, the splinters of which are largely ignored by a contemporary Christian world eager to tell mostly the good part of the story.

The good part, of course, is the love of God in sending his Son to die such a painful death for us. How much he must love and value us to do this! But are these the only messages the cross brings to us? Is it only a coincidence that we receive other versions of these messages from our culture in the form of self-worth and self-love? Has the gospel found us and reoriented our thinking about ourselves to bring it more in line with the truth, or have we merely isolated the parts of the gospel that fit in well with prevailing culture?

What about sin and the helpless state of our existence that sent God's Son to the cross in the first place? In our day, such conviction has been overshadowed by discussions of dysfunction and codependency. Even in our churches, we don't need the cross as much as we need a good psychiatrist to help us straighten out our thinking.

And what about God's inapproachable righteousness and holiness that required a sacrifice for sin? The God of present-day evangelicalism is a big buddy in the sky, and the closest thing to sacrifice most of us understand is a fly ball to right with a runner on third and less than two outs.

What about the blood of bulls and goats that were slaughtered for hundreds of years in a repetitious attempt to satisfy the righteous judgment of God? What do we hear of these things? Do we wonder at all about any of this, or is a contemporary Christian love song from God all we need to know about the cross? Is the cross only a way that

God says, "I love you" to all of us?

The truth is, the timelessness of the cross forces us to encounter many unpleasant realities about ourselves, outside our present cultural mindset. But we may not encounter any of these things in the crosses we see every day—unless we happened into a certain church in Old Greenwich, Connecticut. There an unreasonable ten-foot wooden cross demands to be more than an ornament, a piece of jewelry, a religious icon, or an afterthought.

It's not a particularly memorable church. It uses a good deal of natural wood in the walls and ceiling, but the overall feeling of this building is humble and unpretentious. The platform is low, the floor is concrete, and when I was there last, there were folding chairs set out for the people. The only thing unusual about this church—other than the cross in the middle—is a wide aisle, also down the middle, that is necessary to allow people sitting on either side of the congregation to see around the cross to whomever is standing behind it in the center of the platform.

I was there for a day of seminars, so I was able to experience both sides of the cross—to stand on the platform and talk around the cross to the people and to sit in the congregation and listen around it to the person doing the presentation. And I noticed that it doesn't make much difference where you are. The cross has a leveling effect. It puts us all on the same plane. Teacher/student, performer/audience, pastor/parish, the usual distinctions fall away in the presence of this visual aid. Suddenly we are all in the same boat. No matter what side we are on, the cross always reminds us of our sin, the equality of our guilt, and our only hope.

And the truest hope of the gospel is that forgiveness is available for all of us because we are all sinners of comparable merit. We are, all of us, experts at the subtleties of sin and equally good at cover-up. A cross in the middle of everything blows our cover. It's difficult to be haughty and proud when a hard physical reminder of what that pride cost the Savior casts a shadow in your own personal spotlight.

Something about the cross set in the concrete in Old Greenwich, Connecticut, also reminds me that our salvation is rooted in history. As the familiar hymns tell us, it's an old rugged cross we cling to and an old, old story we tell. To a society that is always trying to reinvent itself, the cross and the gospel appear to be strangely out of sync. Something tells me it's supposed to be this way, that it always was and always will be this way.

The cross shows little regard for relevancy in any age. While each generation tries to manifest its own culture, the cross seems hardly to care. At any point in history, at any place on this planet, the death of Christ, like the lines of the cross itself, runs perpendicular to the flow of culture. The cross is shocking, arresting, out of step, out of time—and yet for all time.

I'm beginning to believe that God designed it this way—that the cross is purposely irrelevant to any age—so that God might draw attention to his sacrifice by virtue of its ageless incongruity. Blood sacrifice for sin doth not a popular song make. And yet the church today is trying to win friends and influence people by being popular and relevant to current needs and trends. To such a church, a stark rendering of the cross in the middle of everything could be an embarrassment.

I travel the country almost every weekend and often spend Sunday in churches far away from home. Perhaps it's just the nature of the particular churches that bring me in, but I am amazed at how contemporary most church services have become. Having been a pioneer of the movement toward more contemporary Christian music, I should welcome this perspective. But somewhere deep inside I wonder if all that contemporary Christian music has brought to the church is necessarily good.

I honestly can't think of the last time I was in an evangelical church that did not have a contemporary worship band and a few singers to help lead the congregation in a rousing session of contemporary music made up of singable, repetitive choruses and danceable rhythms. It seems like years since I've heard an organ.

I grew up in a church that smelled old. The floors creaked when you walked on them. It seemed as if God had been living there for a long time. And when they played music in that church, it creaked, too. It was music you wouldn't hear anywhere else but in church. It wasn't popular music; it was church music. It wasn't supposed to be popular—it didn't have to be. No one was pretending to be trendy about faith. Faith wasn't trendy. It was important—necessary—but certainly not trendy. Faith tied you to something old then, more than to anything new.

When we sang hymns, they were filled with old words—ways to say things that no one said anymore: "Leaning, leaning, /Safe and secure from all alarms; /Leaning, leaning, /Leaning on the everlasting arms." We sang about sailing through bloody seas, about having thousands of tongues to sing with, about marching to Zion.

I don't want to go back. But sometimes I wonder if we went too far too fast or let go of too much in the process of reaching out to our culture. New movements are primarily a reaction to a deficiency in the current state of affairs, and often, in their reactionary nature, they carry their own kind of one-sided blindness. History's movements always swing like pendulums.

Twenty years ago there was a crying need for an expression of faith relevant to the issues of the day. Contemporary Christianity sought to answer that call. Now a different need gnaws at my own soul. It's a need for history, for roots, for substance. As the church today gets increasingly popular—more and more need-oriented, responding to the buttons that people push in their pews—I find myself longing for a historical faith. I find myself not wanting to have everything explained to me in simple terms. I'm not sure I want the paraphrase anymore, not sure I want the mystery solved.

Why was a sacrifice necessary in the first place? Why does there have to be a cross? Why do I find myself longing even for the poetic beauty of King James English that left me wondering? Why do I find myself wanting to go back to hearing an organ again? No, not a glorious pipe organ in a four-thousand-seat auditorium, but one of those ugly-sounding electric ones with someone's grandmother struggling through all four verses of a two-hundred-year-old hymn as we try to sing our way through ancient words that somehow capture, if only for a moment, the mystery of the knowledge of God.

I'm not even sure I want all my needs met as much as I want to meet God, and sometimes I wonder if he's really interested in the noise of our contemporary clamoring. I wonder if we are like my dog, who can't seem to get anywhere because he keeps having to stop and scratch his fleas. I wonder if we are so busy scratching where everybody itches that we aren't taking anybody anywhere significant.

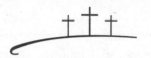

I spent a decade of summers at the Christian Artists Seminar in the Rockies, an annual seminar for contemporary Christian musicians in the mountains of Colorado. When I think back on those days, I try to capture what stands out in my memory. And what stands alone among all the new groups vying for attention was the day Cynthia Clawson sang without any accompaniment: "There is a fountain filled with blood, /Drawn from Emmanuel's veins; /And sinners plunged beneath that flood, /Lose all their guilty stains."

I remember wanting it all to stop right there. I didn't want to hear another musical sound—not another word— for about three days. I just wanted to let that last song echo around in the rocky mountains of my mind until I could hear it no more. I remember resenting the people who got up next to sing—I'm sure they were wonderful. But everything after that mysterious, culturally irrelevant, historical relic of a hymn was mere noise to me. I didn't want to hear another up-tempo expression of the gospel. I wanted to sit for a while with the shocking thought of a fountain of blood spewing from the Savior's veins; I wanted to explore the bizarre thought that this might fill up a dark red pool into which some crazy saint or sinner like me might want to actually plunge his whole body. Nothing about this concept was appealing. Everything about it was arresting and somewhat offensive, as the cross has always been.

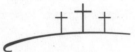

The cross is an anomaly. It is inconsistent with what would naturally be expected. The cross destroys the wisdom of the wise and frustrates the intelligence of the intelligent. Yet it is perfectly in line with a God who has always been full of surprises. Who but God would ever have thought of this, and who but someone he chose would ever believe it?

The very anomaly of the cross, in fact, makes the truth of Christianity self-evident. No human being would have come up with dying on the cross as a means of saving the world. "For since in the wisdom of God the world through its wisdom did not know him, God was pleased through the foolishness of what was preached [the message of the cross] to save those who believe" (1 Corinthians 1:21).

This is why something valuable is lost when the cross becomes no more than a charm or an ornament or a sign a nervous batter makes before an 0 and 2 pitch. This is why the attractive cross on the front wall of the church—the one designed by the same graphic artists who coordinated it with the logo on the bulletin and the four-color brochure that is handed out every Sunday to new visitors—has somehow lost its foolishness. This cross is too pretty. It blends in too well with the decor. It doesn't move us to ask any hard questions like: *Why was it necessary? What does it mean? What is its purpose in my life now?*

The Old Greenwich cross seems more like what crosses should be if we are, in fact, going to have any of them around as reminders. It is rugged, sturdy, hard, bare, and in the way.

The Old Greenwich cross has to be reckoned with. It is in the middle of everything—weddings, funerals, concerts, baptisms, dedications, prayer meetings, Sunday morning services. Where do you put the casket? Are the bride and groom going to stand on either side of it? What if the bride's dress gets caught on a splinter? Where do you put the horn section? Where do you stand? Every event that takes place in this church has to accommodate this cross in some way. It cannot be moved easily like the pulpit or the platform chairs or the Communion table or the planters of ivy that line the platform's edge. It's almost as if the church was built around this cross—as if it were the first thing down before the walls went up and the roof went on.

Something tells me it was.

2

TRUE COLORS

IN CASE YOU HAVEN'T NOTICED, we seem to have acquired a new evangelical God. He does not burn with the fire of judgment or shine with the blinding white light of unapproachable righteousness. His Son is not stained with the blood of the sacrifice, nor are his followers aware of any blood on their own hands that would put them in need of such a sacrifice. He is in every way a kinder, gentler God, much more in touch with the real "felt needs" of people than he ever has been. No longer sinners before an angry God, we are winners with a Cosmic Cheerleader. This God is fashionable, and he matches the prevailing color of his newer sanctuaries that are springing up across the land. This is the new evangelical God for a new century. Color him mauve.

It's been a long time coming. For most of history, God has not been very popular. For some reason, in the past he has been more inclined to choose the weak things over the strong, the lowly and despised things—the things that are not—that he might nullify the things that are. And his message has been thought of as foolishness by most of the people. He even used to say that the fear of him was the first step in finding him. Imagine that! It is no wonder so few have been able to follow him, even when his Son was here. Of course, all that has changed now that God has adopted mauve as his color.

This is especially exciting news for his ministers. They can finally put behind them the maligning they used to get from the world and preach a gospel of truly good news— news that everyone will be eager to hear: *God really does like us; he accepts us just as we are.* Those old scary messages about sin and guilt and judgment and the cross were only old-fashioned ways of telling people that what God really wants is for them to feel good about themselves. People don't need to concern themselves with those old notions any longer—all that about judging sin and dying on the cross. That was all God's business—theological stuff he had to deal with so he could be nice to us. But now that it's over, people don't need to hear about any of that uncomfortable stuff anymore. All they need to know is that God likes them now and has wonderful plans for their lives. After all, he created everyone, you know, and "God don't make no junk!" That's the bottom line.

It's easy to see why this mauve God fits in so much better with our culture than he used to. God's new color has even made church popular with people who previously wouldn't have been interested in coming anywhere near a place where he was supposed to be found. People are going to church in droves now, because, maybe for the first time in history, church has something to do with the real issues people face, such as managing finances, overcoming bad relationships, finding better ones, parenting, conquering addictions, getting healed, breaking free of codependencies, eating right, and taking care of their bodies. God has always been involved in bringing healing and hope to people's lives, of course—but now that seems to be the primary focus of our concern. Why, church is almost as good as a good shrink.

Even what people have to do to become Christians now is so much easier than it used to be before God was mauve. Used to be you had to realize you were a helpless sinner facing the impossible demands of a holy God. You had to despair of anything you could ever do or be and throw yourself upon his mercy and hope he might find some remote reason to be favorably disposed to you when you knew good and well you deserved the worst. But that was when God was blinding white and his Son was stained with red and there was blood on our hands.

That's all changed now. All we need to do now to become a Christian is open up the door of our heart, and Christ will come in. And with such a kind, cool, mauve God waiting harmlessly on the other side of the door, that shouldn't threaten anyone. What a comfort it must be to people, what a surprise to discover that after being afraid to open that door for so long, they had no more reason to fear God than they would fear Mister Rogers.

Nope, there's nothing quite like knowing that Jesus died to make me happy. He died for me, he lives for me, and he's just waiting for me to come around. How could anyone leave such a nice God out there in the cold?

It's truly a great time to serve God and spread his Word to the world, isn't it? It all blends so well. No one will think you are foolish anymore. God's colors have never been so *in*!

There's one small problem, however. I haven't been able to find "mauve" anywhere in the Bible. I'm still looking, but so far it hasn't turned up. Instead, I keep seeing red. Red as in the color of blood. Red as in the color of sin. "Though your sins are like scarlet, they shall be as white as snow; though they are red as crimson, they shall be like wool" (Isaiah 1:18).

Much of the Old Testament—and a lot of the New, in fact—is stained in red. This is not good news for our trendy mauve gospel. No color will stop people in their tracks faster than red. Real red. Blood red. No one bleeds *rose*. They bleed *red*, like Jesus did—because of our sin.

Red is an arresting color, especially on someone else. When we see blood on ourselves, we automatically go into a state of shock, which cushions our reactions, but on someone else, we are often repulsed by what we see. I have a recurring fear when I'm driving the L.A. freeways that sooner or later I am going to be the first at the scene of a serious traffic accident. I imagine someone pinned under a car—while hundreds of gawking motorists pass on by— and I struggle hypothetically with whether I would care enough to stop and help. I imagine someone's life flowing out on the street, and I wonder what I would do. I almost think I would rather be the victim of a terrible accident— rather shed my own blood—than to be whole and healthy and witness such an ugly scene.

What was it like, I wonder, to see Christ bleed—to watch the thick red life flow out of him and turn dark as it slowly seeped into the brown dirt around the cross—to want to put it back and not be able to do anything about it?

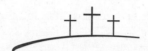

The wounds on his hands bled slowly. Pressure from the weight of his body held back the flow. If there had been no other sounds that afternoon, it probably would have sounded like the slow, steady drip off the eaves of a mountain cabin on a damp, foggy night.

But there were many sounds. Taunts from the soldiers, weeping and wailing from the women near the feet of Jesus, even careless laughter from children playing haphazardly around the perimeter of the crucifixion hill, oblivious to the significance of this particular execution. Small dark puddles would gather briefly under the top beam of the cross, only to be covered by the shuffle of a guard's feet. And then it would start in again: drip . . . drip . . . drip—little droplets seen but not heard.

Mary saw them. She stared at the puddle through her bloodshot eyes while his life flashed before her, and it seemed to her that the earth swallowed his blood as if it had been created for this. As if it were drinking its fill and would thirst no more.

Then she slowly turned her eyes up to his face, and her breath failed her. He already had her in the grasp of his eyes. It was the first time he had looked at her from the cross, and his eyes were full of the deepest despair and the deepest love she had ever known. It seemed as if she were falling—falling into a bottomless abyss. She looked until she could bear it no more and turned her eyes away so she could catch her breath again. Once more her gaze went to the small puddle in the dirt, and it seemed now that she, and only she, could hear the droplets landing, loud enough to shut out all other sounds.

Then she heard his words spoken to her: "Dear woman, here is your son." And to the disciple he loved, "Here is your mother."

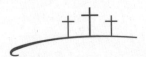

A second cross stands tall at the Presbyterian church of Old Greenwich, Connecticut. This one is outside, near the front of the church, clearly visible from the street and from the railway lines. Trains pass within view of it a dozen times a day, carrying commuters to and from New York City.

Because of this high visibility, the architect desired to make a statement with this second cross as well. This would be a different statement—a public statement for those out-side the church. This cross he made of steel. Not stainless steel, but a kind of raw steel that would stain profusely and reveal its rugged character even from a distance.

When the architect planned this cross, he was thinking of the natural look it would have from the train or the street. The cross would take on earthy tones that would change with the weather. He wanted to project a real cross, scarred by time, not something shiny, cold, and refined. He had worked with this material before and knew how it responded to the elements—how unpredictable it was and yet how warm the tones would be. But the most significant aspect about this outdoor cross never occurred to him.

When it rains, this cross drips red. Rust-red. It is probably his most powerful image. The concrete under the cross is now permanently stained, and each time it rains, the cement receives a fresh new splattering. In winter, when the sun comes out and heats up the cross after a storm, the slow melting from it drips rust-red holes in the pure white snow.

Jesus Christ died a violent death. The Bible is a bloody book. This is not pleasant stuff to talk about, and yet I wonder how capable we are of grasping the meaning behind these powerful pictures without encountering their reality in some way.

That reality woke me up the other day. I was casually reading from my Bible over a bowl of Honey Nut Cheerios, and I found carnage. I mean, it was a bloody mess. I wouldn't even have been reading this if it weren't for these annual Bible reading schedules that force me to separate pages in the Old Testament that are still stuck together even though I've had my Bible for years.

We don't often hear sermons or testimonies out of Leviticus. Imagine someone sharing his favorite Scripture verse, Leviticus 4:4: "He is to present the bull at the entrance to the Tent of Meeting before the Lord. He is to lay his hand on its head and slaughter it before the Lord." I'm sure we'd all be anxious to meet this person after church!

And so I sat there with my cereal getting soggy, thinking about being a priest and looking forward to a day of slaughtering bulls and goats and lambs. He spent his day removing their hides, separating their organs and fat, cutting them into pieces—wringing the heads and tearing the wings off doves—and constantly sprinkling blood everywhere: on altars, and toes, and earlobes of other priests. Imagine the stench, the sight of all that blood, the flies, the mess. And imagine, most of all, that it never stops. A priest just finishes with one bull, and someone comes up to him with another one and says, "Would you please sacrifice El Toro here? I just had an affair with my neighbor's wife."

If I were a priest, I'd want to take my knife to him instead. "Why didn't you think of that before you started fooling around?" I would be tempted to say. After all, what does this guy's personal life have to do with a poor innocent bull?

Imagine these priests, all day long immersed in blood and guts and fire—on a hot, humid day in the Sinai, no less. Suddenly, as I read Leviticus over my bowl of cereal, I saw this practice from a priest's point of view. The people kept on sinning, and priests kept on cutting into warm flesh. Sinning and ripping open and sprinkling and burning and sinning and ripping open and sprinkling and burning and sinning and . . .

Don't you think at some point one of them might have raised his sticky hands toward heaven and shouted over all the moos and the bleats and the cooing: "Will you people *please* stop all this *sinning!*"

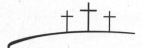

More soldiers came to the execution site with fresh orders from headquarters. Most of the crowd had left; only a small contingent of family and friends remained huddled near the cross in the center. It was strangely quiet now. Anyone could have heard the dripping from the crossbar had the blood not already thickened and dried on his hands. The dripping had stopped minutes before, right after the earth shook and Jesus cried out with a voice that nearly stopped Mary's heart. Then all had gone still except for the sucking, sporadic breathing coming from the other two criminals.

"This one's already dead," said one of the guards. "Can you believe that?"

"He was a weak one," said another.

"No need to break his legs, I guess."

"Well, just to make sure..." One of them approached the dead body of Jesus with his spear, and before Mary could scream out, "No!" he thrust its tip up into the torso of the Son of God just under the ribs. Her scream and the sudden flow of blood and water came out at the same time.

Disgusted, the guard wiped a few drops from his face and walked away.

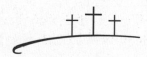

From cleaning quail on a hunting trip, or maybe from driving past freshly flattened small animal sacrifices along the highway, I know what it smells like when something living is cut open. It's a horrible smell. Blood is repulsive. Many people faint at the mere sight of it. Most of us feel lucky that we hardly ever have to encounter the smell or the sight of blood.

But today, after reading Leviticus, I wonder if it's lucky after all. We miss something of the consequences of sin, something of the cross, by being so isolated from this painful object lesson—something of what it really costs to buy our forgiveness, something of what it really costs to sin.

The cross in Connecticut that drips rust-red is significant because it is still bleeding, just as somehow my sin makes Christ bleed. It is an unfathomable present tense connection with a past event. Christ died once, but somehow, perhaps outside the realms of time and space, my present sin, even sins I have yet to commit, make their own contribution to his death.

Sin and blood have always been tied together in the mind of God. My sin has to have a payment. Either I pay for it with my own blood, or someone else has to pay it for me—a bull or a lamb, over and over, or the final, perfect Lamb. No one gets to walk without someone bleeding.

I have no more right to dodge the reality of this than the person in Leviticus who had to repeatedly haul in a new animal to the priest. Yet we both have tried. I know enough about the development of religion to guess how they got out of facing the unpleasant aspects of this practice. I bet in time, the priests got tired of being splattered with fresh blood and hired someone else to do the job for them so they could keep their hands and robes clean. After all, they had an image to maintain.

And I imagine it wasn't long before you could drop off your animal at a special gate in the back of the temple, like the claims department of an insurance company, and everything would be taken care of for you, neat and clean. Wealthy ranchers probably had someone pick up a lamb for them on a regular basis, for a nominal fee. (Levites had to make a living, too, you know.) Real simple and efficient.

It's not too much different now. We have a way of making perfunctory that which should be graphic in our lives. Sin, confession, forgiveness, are all bloody and painful, even painfully joyful if we fully embrace them. But instead, we like to keep most of this in the abstract. "On a hill far away..." we keep the reality of Christ's death—and our own sin—distant, liturgical, even theological... anything but personal.

But if Jesus Christ died for the sins of the world, then those sins committed *after* his death are just as responsible for putting him on a cross as the sins committed *before*. This truth makes it hard to love Jesus and knowingly transgress the law of God. It's like saying you love someone while you are twisting a knife in his back—the ultimate in mixed messages.

Seeing the cause and effect between my present tense sin and Christ's past tense death might mean I will have to do something about sinning beyond casually accepting God's grace.

I wonder how much carnage we create without really knowing it. I wonder if it might make a difference in my life if, when I went to the pastor's office to confess a sin, he would have to wrestle a bull from the closet and start slicing away.

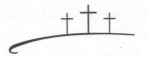

It's a good thing red is not the only color in the Bible. White is a color, too. "Though your sins are like scarlet, they shall be as white as snow" (Isaiah 1:18). White is the color of forgiveness, the color of robes and garments and hearts made pure, the color of horses in Revelation and fine linen on priestly clothes, the color of a great throne at the end of time, upon which God will sit and judge the world.

White is the absence of sin. It is a heart without blemish, pure as new snow. It's hard to believe that white is the color of my heart, and yours, through Christ. It's not a simple thing, though. White was bought at the price of red.

White is also the color of bright light that always accompanies God's glory. The clothes Jesus wore when he was joined on the mountain of transfiguration with Moses and Elijah turned as white as the light around him. And the angel, who made that stunning Garden announcement to the women who came to anoint his body, was dressed in the same glowing white as well.

Black is a biblical color, too. It's the color you get if you mix all the primary colors together on a palette. Black is the darkness that I was born into. It is the color of my heart apart from saving grace. Black is the tunnel I stare into when I try to find my own way out of things. Black was the color of the night when God's Son was announced to the world, shattering the hold darkness held on a Palestinian hillside and ushering in the true light at the end of every-one's tunnel.

Black was also the color of the sky when Christ died, and black is the darkness that awaits those who have invaded the fold of believers but feed only themselves. False teachers—"wandering stars, for whom blackest darkness has been reserved forever" (Jude 13).

Green are the plants and the herbs he gave us to enjoy for food, healing, and the enjoyment of sheer beauty. Green are the trees that clap their hands and the mountains that break forth into singing. Green is to plants what red is to us—the life-flow that feeds them and makes a hillside shimmer with delight. It is the light green, velvety, vulnerable shade of a brand new leaf, or the opaque dark green of an old, musty summer. It is the color of the evergreen that brings hope even in the cold, dark winter; and at Christmastime, in the holly leaf, it sets off the red berry with a contrast that makes it glow with plump merriment.

Green was the grass upon which a multitude sat and were fed with the bread and fish that kept coming out of a young boy's small lunch bag.

God does mess with pastels from time to time—in a mauve California sunset or the soft shades of a tropical orchid. But it seems he's mostly into primary colors.

Primarily red. And most of all, the scenes from Leviticus and the outdoor cross haunt me. They won't let go. Their images live on and stain the walls of my mind with rust-red drops of rain.

3

THE MYSTERY OF THE CROSS

THE EIGHTEENTH-CENTURY IRISH philosopher George J. Berkeley believed that to exist meant to be perceived. He was the first to postulate that if a tree fell in the forest and there was no one there to hear it fall, there was a question as to whether it actually made noise when it fell or not. This seemingly silly question started a major epistemological debate by a number of brilliant minds as to the validity of the sounds of falling trees in the forests of the world. Berkeley's ultimate conclusion was that the falling tree did make a sound even though no one was there to hear it, because, in fact, God heard it. God hears everything.

Something akin to this debate presents itself in the case of the cross. Jesus Christ died at a moment in history, like a tree that fell in a forest, but no one heard—at least no one you or I know personally. The debate about Christ's death on the cross and its personal relevance to you or me may go on indefinitely, but the significance of the cross and its purpose in the world is unaltered by what we happen to think about it. Jesus Christ's death on a cross does not have to be ratified by anyone. It does not have to be understood to be true. The gospel does not have to move me emotionally before it can save me. The Son of God died on a real wooden cross on a rocky hillside in human history for the sins of the world. You and I were not there to see it or hear it, but God saw it, and therein lies its primary significance.

This perspective is sorely missing today in a Christianity that works so hard to make itself acceptable on a personal level. In an attempt to simplify the gospel, to make the gospel make sense to minds that do not want to have to adjust very much to understand it, we have selected those parts of it that are compatible with popular culture. And we have assumed we were doing God a big favor by getting this concept down to a level where so many folks can follow along. In an attempt to get people to accept Jesus as their personal Savior, we are altering the picture of Jesus we present, in order to make it more easily acceptable.

I sometimes wonder if we haven't become guilty of doing what Jesus warned us against: giving what is sacred to dogs and casting pearls in front of pigs. Are we devaluing the gospel by attempting to make it attractive to people who are not interested in following it in the first place and wouldn't recognize it even if it turned up in their trough? Have we cast away the grain of the gospel with the cornhusks of commercialism? Are we not now reaping the very consequences Jesus predicted, as we witness the gospel being trampled and torn apart by those who possess no real desire to understand and know God?

I fear we have made the individual experience of the believer paramount to everything else. What's important is that *I* see and hear the tree fall. It's no longer important merely that it happened, it's important that it happens *to me*. We have a gospel that is first for me before it is for anyone else, even God, and thus it appears that God goes dancing about to please my latest whim or fad in hopes that the gospel might strike my fancy if the emotion is right. Thus we have God trying to market himself to the felt needs of people, and unfortunately, I don't think he's doing a very good job. Not only are we inclined to feel sorry for a man who died on a cross, we also have a tendency to feel sorry for his God who is trying everything he can think of to get people to find this an attractive thought in the twenty-first century. The cross is a hard sell to this generation unless we soften it somehow or remove it all together.

Of course, God is not in the least bit concerned with any of these games or ploys. These are only errors in the way we perceive Christianity, but if we defined God by our perception, this picture of him would not be that far from the truth. Meanwhile, the Son of God died on the cross like a tree falling in a forest when no one was around to hear the crash.

"I'm sorry to disturb you, Pilate, but there's someone here to see you . . . says he wants to do something with the body."

"What body? Don't you know it's after hours? Send him back tomorrow."

"The body of that Jewish messiah," said the temple guard with the slur of a man who had already started on his happy hour before he left the office. Pilate looked at him with disgust. He would have ripped the man's job out from under him right then and there if he hadn't been one of Caesar's appointments. All of his problems, it seemed to Pilate, were Caesar's appointments.

"I wouldn't have bothered you except that he is a rather prominent man from Arimathea. I'm sure he will make it worth your while," he said, patting his coin belt and pulling back his lips to reveal a Cheshire-cat smile fat with the feathers of its own fresh bribe.

"All right. Bring me my robe and send him in. Wait a minute . . . you aren't talking about that Jesus character, are you? The one we crucified this afternoon?"

"Yes," said the temple guard, as Pilate's personal valet helped him into his robe. "That's the one."

"Impossible. No one dies that quickly on a cross. Have you any confirmation?"

"No, sir."

"Well, I'm certainly not going to give anyone the body of a criminal without confirmation of death. Get me the centurion in charge of today's operation." He waved the guard away.

"Jesus . . . the 'King of the Jews,'" he reminded himself under his breath. "Will I ever be done with this man?"

Pilate adjusted his robe and strolled to the window while the footsteps of the guard disappeared down the hall. It seemed to him that the sun went down early on this day. It was one day he would just as soon forget anyway. He wondered why it felt like the middle of the night.

"Gaius," he said to his valet, "what time is it?"

"It's time to close the office, sir."

"But why is it so dark?"

"It's been this way since the middle of the afternoon, sir. I don't know why. Nothing but dark clouds without rain."

Suddenly a centurion guard appeared at the entrance to the room.

"How did you get here so fast? Why aren't you at the site? What's going on here? Am I the only person who knows it's not the middle of the night?"

"Sir, we left the site an hour ago. I gave most of the men the night off. We broke the legs of two of them. They'll scream all night. Strangest thing, though. The other one is already dead."

"The Jew?"

"Yes, sir."

"Will you vouch for that?"

"Sir, I personally shoved my spear right up to his heart. He was dead. No breath. No movement. Strangest thing: Blood and water came out. Never saw that before."

"Blood and water?" Pilate walked back to the window and thought. Lots of things were happening today that people had never seen before. What was going on?

"How many guards are there now?"

"Two, sir. The crowd has fairly dispersed. Only a couple of women crying over the dead one."

"Very well. You may go. Guard, bring me Mr. Fat Belt from Arimathea."

The temple guard flashed his toothy smile again, but Pilate only stared at him.

"Thank you, Your Honor, for seeing me after hours," Joseph said nervously as he hurried into the room. "I am prepared to make it worth—"

"No need. I have already washed my hands of this matter, and I do not wish to dirty them again. What is it you want?"

"We would like the body of Jesus of Nazareth for burial. I have a tomb on my property already prepared."

"Why tonight? He can come down tomorrow with the others."

"Your Honor, if you would, please. Our custom is that no work be done on the Sabbath. Today is our Day of Preparation. I have made all the proper arrangements. I will take care of everything."

Pilate looked at Joseph's clothes and wondered what interest a well-to-do businessman would have in a poor country preacher whose luck had obviously run out.

"Are you related to him?"

Joseph hesitated and then surprised himself with what on the one hand was a lie but on the other was the most certain truth he had ever spoken.

"Yes."

"All right. You may have your dead man, but you will have two guards with you to ensure that the body gets put in that tomb and sealed properly. Guard, fetch me the centurion again!"

There is an underlying assumption in contemporary Christianity that needs to be reexamined—the assumption that a message spoken in a manner relevant to culture will give the message a better chance of being both heard and accepted. A popular person becoming a Christian and giving his testimony will make more people want to become Christians. Or a message sung to contemporary sounds and rhythms, couched in lyrics salted with current phrases, will attract more people to it.

I would never argue with the first premise. A contemporary packaging of the gospel will definitely be heard by more people than would a culturally archaic form. When I first started writing and singing contemporary songs of faith, I had an immediate hearing with my generation. The rapport was instant. But hearing and accepting are not the same thing. Not only is there a question as to whether people who hear this popular form of the message all embrace it; the larger question is: *What are they accepting if they do embrace the message?* Is it the same one we think we're giving? Is it the gospel? Is it Jesus Christ they are responding to— the one who lived in history and died on a cross?

And what if there is nothing in popular culture to which the gospel message can be relevant? What if the gospel is incompatible with our culture as we know it today? How do we know if the message we think we are bringing is even being heard? What if culture speaks so loudly that it drowns out the gospel every time? What if the essence of popular American culture is actually embodied in a tabloid or a soap opera? How are we going to make the gospel relevant to that? Should we even try?

In 1970, when Larry Norman sang, *"Why don't you look into Jesus, he's got the answer,"* the song was relevant because in 1970 a lot of people were "looking into" things. Today, few people are looking into anything. Looking into something indicates a contemplation of sorts. It implies an intellectual search for meaning that was part of the popular culture when Larry wrote this song. Videos of audiences in the early seventies show them surprisingly calm compared to audiences today. They sat there and listened—even to hard rock. They contemplated. They observed. They were thinking about it as well as experiencing it

Tell an audience to look into Jesus today, and they probably would wonder where you wanted them to look: at the video screen... at the scaffolding... at the stage— which one? Is he coming in by helicopter? Parachute? Perhaps he's on a roving camera? And who is Jesus anyway, a new talk-show host? "Hey, are we on live? Is that him? He's got a microphone!"

Today's audience might be best described as cartoonist Bill Watterson portrays it in *Calvin and Hobbes*. Calvin is bowing down to the television set and crying out, "Oh, great altar of passive entertainment, bestow upon me thy discordant images at such speed as to render linear thought impossible!" In another cartoon, Calvin decides to believe in astrology and horoscopes, especially when he can take their prophecies to mean whatever he wants. He concludes his contemporary apologetic by stating: "The newspaper couldn't print it if it weren't true!"

Society today is a consumer market, not given to much thought about anything—a society with myriad answers to choose from, any one of them as true as the next. This society does not question or contemplate meaning; it merely records data much as one would absorb sixty channels of cable TV all at once. It is a society incapable of making any lasting value judgments; whatever is printed or flashed on the screen is true.

If Christianity were printed in Calvin's world, it would

be accepted on the same level as the horoscope, and Christians who misunderstand this about our culture would think that the gospel was making great strides in the comic pages. It should be pretty clear by now that most "television ministry" has become merely one more channel of passive entertainment.

In such a culture, an irrelevant message may convey the truth more clearly and accurately than a relevant one. Anything relevant to this culture is going to run the chance of getting lost in the crowd. In front of this backdrop, the irrelevancy of a man who was executed two thousand years ago because he said he came from God might be just the thing to get everyone's attention.

By trying to make the gospel culturally relevant, we may be operating at cross-purposes to God and canceling out the very effectiveness of the truth. God has always preferred to put his messages at odds with the world. More often than not, he slants his messages counterculturally. He works against the grain. He sets out to save the world through a remnant of cultural outcasts who never seem to be able to get their own act together, so much so that they kill off the very man for whom they have been waiting for thousands of years. Then God announces that his death, believe it or not, will save them and everybody else, too.

All along, of course, God introduced this plan through a line of prophets who were never welcomed in their own day. And he even goes on to say that those who follow his message today will find themselves facing an equally hostile audience. Perhaps we are running against God's intended purposes when we try to make becoming a Christian the exciting, culturally relevant thing to do. If becoming a

Christian suddenly becomes popular, we have to wonder if this is the same Christianity Jesus was talking about.

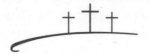

We don't have to read much further than Paul's statement that the preaching of the cross is foolishness to man to realize that no matter how attractive we make this package, the message it contains is going to be a hard sell among current ways of thinking.

Jesus Christ came out of nowhere. He was a man for all times, at home in none of them. He came to make visible what was invisible. Jesus Christ brought the eternal truths of God into the arena of daily human life and culture, but he was not enmeshed in that culture. He was not defined by first-century Roman life. His life and his message transcended his culture.

Simultaneously, Jesus stood both inside and outside of culture. This ability of the gospel to transform as well as transcend—to stand outside of culture as well as inside—is the aspect of the gospel that our present contemporary efforts lack. We are too much "in" to be able to lead anyone "out."

Pilate sent Joseph and the head centurion away, hoping to be finally done with the ordeal. He had a strong urge to wash his hands again but ignored it. "Leave me alone for a few minutes," he said to Gaius, and he slumped down into his chair, rubbing his eyes. Suddenly the memory of Jesus standing before him only hours before sprang to his mind, and he heard every word again.

"Are you the king of the Jews?"

"Is that your own idea, or did others talk to you about me?" The audacity of this man, speaking to him like that! Pilate had wanted to strike him, but something constrained him. That strange warning message from his wife, the dreams . . .

Pilate did remember reacting to Jesus by saying, *"Am I a Jew?"* He liked that. It was a smart thing to have said, he thought. Almost as smart as when he deposited his brilliant question: *"What is truth?"* and then left without an answer.

"It was your people and your chief priests who handed you over to me. What is it you have done, anyway?"

"My kingdom is not of this world." Pilate recalled the prisoner's words, and as he sat at his desk and reviewed the events of this strange day, he had to admit that he almost believed the man. What kind of king would find himself in his hour of need abandoned by all his followers? If he was a king, it certainly wasn't of any place in or around Pilate's jurisdiction.

Pilate was more than prepared to cross Jesus off as just another nut case—and that is, indeed, what he would do. God knows he'd seen enough of them in his rule. But that was just the problem. He'd seen too many nut cases—too many to be able to pass this one off as just one more. If this man was crazy, he was crazy in a most intelligent way, for Pilate had never heard anyone speak this way before. This man was too smart. There was something different about him—something that made Pilate almost believe it when he said he was from some other world.

"My kingdom is not of this world." Pilate muttered the words to himself, and suddenly he imagined Joseph pulling the dead body of the king of the Jews down from the cross. He chuckled lightly. His kingdom was sure enough not of this world anymore. His followers had seen to that.

Take the message of the cross—nothing could be more countercultural. But even this gaping scar on the hillside of history can, in the interest of making a more acceptable message to today's audience, be turned into nothing more arresting than a precious moment.

I asked God, "How much do you love me?" and he stretched out his arms on the cross and said, "This much." This popular poster found in many churches and Christian homes is true to a point. But it is not the whole story. This lovely picture of Jesus dying for me is touching—but *why* is he doing this? Why is he up there in the first place? Why do I need somebody to die for me? I didn't realize I was in so much trouble. Oh, a little dysfunctional maybe; I have a few addictions, but who doesn't? I'm getting good therapy, and I'm even going to church. I listen to Christian radio all the time, and I'm starting to believe in myself. So I'll just put the poster up on my wall and feel good about the fact that God loves me so much that he would do something like this.

I've heard numerous evangelistic messages that say, bottom line, that Jesus died to make good people even better.

The speakers wouldn't have put it quite in those words, but that was the gist of it. But such appeals fall short of the gospel. They put God's love on our terms—the cross as a greeting card personalized to me. Who wouldn't like that?

The passion of Christ can be played out in front of people without putting demands on anyone as long as it is not tied to God's holiness and our own personal sin. It becomes his tragedy at that point, not ours. Most people don't like admitting that their life is a tragedy, but the ongoing success of soap operas suggests that most of us have no problem watching someone else's pain. And to those who fail to face their own tragedies there, the cross becomes God's unfortunate little drama.

As a child I can remember staring into my glass of grape juice during Communion, trying to imagine Christ on the cross and feel sorry for him, or for myself, or just trying to feel sorry in general since everyone else seemed to be so sorry. All those times I came up as empty as that empty little glass I discarded in the ring of wood on the back of the pew in front of me.

The pastor attempted to incite our sorrow by drawing out the physical aspects of the crucifixion—the thorns being pressed into his skull, his back being ripped open by whips with sharp objects in their tails, the nails going into his hands, the cross being lifted and dropped into its hole in the ground wrenching the joints in his body, the dehydration, the spear in the side, the blood, the water—and all of this gruesome pain and agony was dramatized as the fullest expression of love man has ever known.

Love and execution. What strange bedfellows!

If that same pastor were suddenly surrounded by a

swarm of military personnel who rushed the room, nailed him to a cross, and dropped it down into the floor in front of us with him on it, I doubt that the first thing in people's minds would be how much he loved them. It wouldn't even be the last thing. The more accurate reaction probably would be "What on earth is going on here?"

The ones who knew Jesus and loved him were probably thinking the same thing on the day he was crucified: "What on earth is going on here?" The ones who didn't were probably thinking, "What a fool!" I doubt there was one person at Golgotha hill that afternoon who felt loved in any way by this gruesome spectacle.

I remember all those times I came up as empty as my Communion glass and wonder if perhaps I wasn't supposed to understand it, after all. Maybe I was just supposed to sit and eat and drink in awe of it—the mystery, that is . . . and the humility.

The mystery shrouding the cross cannot be reduced to something we can completely understand as human beings. The truth of the cross is beyond and behind and before us, bigger than anything we can hold in our hands. Without this mystery, sacrifice turns into sentiment, and substitutionary death into drama. The hard cross softens into a mushy display of God's love for me that doesn't have much more depth than a Barry Manilow love ballad.

Yes, the cross is the ultimate expression of God's love. But it is just that: *God's* love. Not our love. This is a love that we do not understand. It is a love that is completely foreign to the way we operate. No popular song or expression can come close to it.

"You see, at just the right time, when we were still powerless, Christ died for the ungodly. Very rarely will anyone die for a righteous man, though for a good man someone might possibly dare to die. But God demonstrates his own love for us in this: While we were still sinners, Christ died for us" (Romans 5:6–8).

This is God's love. This is how it was demonstrated. We have no human counterpart for such love, no words to express it. Unless our message comes through the cross, our need, and the sacrificial requirement of a holy God, it will be interpreted as something other than what it is.

Much of the Crucifixion is a mystery that lies beyond us. Those bulls and rams and lambs and turtledoves and goats all charred and burning, sending their acrid smoke heavenward as a peculiar, sweet-smelling savor to the nostrils of God—all that was really necessary. And Jesus dying as the final Lamb of God who takes away the sins of the world . . .

I didn't come up with this. To be quite honest, I find the whole idea somewhat repulsive. But I notice that God didn't ask my opinion first. He just did it. He sent his only-begotten Son to die on the cross and announced its importance throughout all the Scriptures from beginning to end, so that those who believed would be saved, just as all who looked upon the serpent that Moses raised on a staff in the wilderness were healed of their deadly diseases.

Those who believed were healed. Not those who were moved to tears, not those who felt loved, not those who wanted to feel sorry for God, but those who believed—believed something they did not even understand, but believed it nonetheless. Believed it because they had no choice. They looked at themselves and saw a deadly disease, and they looked at the provision of God and were healed.

The fact that blood is necessary as a sacrifice for human sin, that it is required of God as a payment, and that Christ's blood is enough to secure the transaction for the whole world, is not up to me to understand. It is not a tender moment to be cherished, but a fact to be believed, a currency required for entry into heaven. There is an exchange policy at work here. We turn over what we know of ourselves for a currency foreign to us but required in the new kingdom we aspire to enter. Thus it is with the sacrificial blood of Jesus. I may not understand it, but I'll gladly take it. As the hymn writer has so simply and profoundly put it:

> I am not skilled to understand
> What God hath willed, what God hath planned;
> I only know at His right hand
> Stands One who is my Savior.
> I take Him at his word and deed:
> "Christ died to save me," this I read;
> And in my heart I find a need
> Of Him to be my Savior.[1]
> —Dora Greenwell

Maybe that's why I'm drawn to these strange crosses as they have been rendered by a bold architect in Old Greenwich, Connecticut. I'm not comfortable around these crosses. They're not easy to accept or dismiss. They do not make me feel warm and fuzzy. They are nothing for which I can find a counterpart elsewhere. There is a mystery and a grace and a wonder and a painful reality attached to them

[1]Dora Greenwell (1821–1882), "I Am Not Skilled to Understand."

that speaks to me of the truth.

The cross was for God first before it was ever for me or anyone else. God was reconciling the world to himself through Christ (2 Corinthians 5:19); God loved the world so much that he gave his only-begotten Son (John 3:16); God demonstrated his love for us by having Christ die for us while we were still sinners (Romans 5:8). Even before Jesus died for you and me, he died for God. He did this for his Father because of what the Father wanted to accomplish through Christ's death; to this end, Christ was obedient unto death, and in that obedience is his greatest glory.

This raises an important question: Did Christ die for me because I was worth buying back, or did Christ die for me because he wanted to display his grace through me to the universe? If redemption hinges on my worth, then God is nothing more than a good businessman: He's getting a good deal on his investment. But if redemption hinges on the display of the totality of God's plan to the rulers and authorities in heavenly places, then we are not the point; we are simply part of a big plan to glorify God. His grace and his mercy as displayed through his church is the point. The point is to bring glory to God—to worship him with every knee and every tongue in the act.

This attitude is described for us in Philippians 2:5–11:

> Christ Jesus: who, being in very nature God, did not consider equality with God something to be grasped, but made himself nothing, taking the very nature of a servant, being made in human likeness. And being found in appearance as a man, he humbled himself and became obedient to death—even death on a cross! Therefore God exalted him to the

highest place and gave him the name that is above every name, that at the name of Jesus every knee should bow, in heaven and on earth and under the earth, and every tongue confess that Jesus Christ is Lord, to the glory of God the Father.

This description of the work of Christ on the cross does not mention anything about *us* except our *knees*; it has everything to do with God and his Son and what Christ's obedience demonstrated about his attitude. We are the by-products of his work, and we will join in the worship. But in degree of importance, I believe Jesus Christ died for God before he died for me. God was foremost on his mind.

In other words, I was not the first reason why God's Son died. His justice and his mercy, and the display of this part of himself to the entire universe, are closer to the first reason why God's Son died than I am. I get to be a small part of a very big picture, and that is a fact I cannot take in all at once. It is a picture so big that much of it still remains a mystery to me. A picture that becomes a deeper mystery the more I look at it. A tree fell in a forest; I wasn't there, but it was extremely important to the tree, to the one who made it, to history, to all the other trees—and thus, finally, to me.

God does not need me to respond to him in order to make all the trouble he went to worth it. What Jesus did is already worth it regardless of me, or you, because the primary reason he died on the cross was to obey his Father in heaven. Any other reason pales in importance.

4

THE BODY OF EVIDENCE

BETTER LATE THAN NEVER, Nicodemus thought as he waited for Joseph to return from his meeting with Pilate. The sky was black with night, and the torches around the crosses cast long flickering shadows over the hillside. Only the shadows danced. The bodies were still, none stiller than the one in the middle. It seemed to him that all time and the world stopped as Jesus hung there in silence.

They had found each other, Joseph and Nicodemus: two wealthy Jews. Too well-connected to risk following Jesus in life, they had finally risen to the occasion now in his death and were prepared to show their allegiance, even if posthumously.

Nicodemus had watched the Crucifixion the way he followed Jesus for the last three years: from a distance. From the olive trees on a rise just beyond the hillside, actually, beyond the perimeter of the crowd. Now in the darkness, he ventured closer.

It made him think of the other time he had visited Jesus under cover of darkness. That conversation had cut deep into his mind so that it was permanently etched on his memory. Now he heard the words again as if for the first time. *"Just as Moses lifted up the snake in the desert, so the Son of Man must be lifted up."*

Now he knew. But the words that stung the most as he crept toward the circle of torches were these: *"This is the verdict: Light has come into the world, but men loved darkness instead of light because their deeds were evil. Everyone who does evil hates the light, and will not come into the light for fear that his deeds will be exposed."*

The cross has always borne a simple and very direct message: There's something wrong with the human race. Something had to be done. Anything short of this message misses the point. We are a dysfunctional people so wrapped and tangled in our iniquity that no amount of therapy can unravel us. There is something fundamentally wrong with us, and we are individually and corporately powerless to fix it.

At the inauguration of the forty-second president of the United States, Billy Graham, evangelist and national spokesperson of God for a generation, was asked to bring the inaugural prayer. I watched as he made his way slowly to the platform, carrying every one of his fifty years of ministry on his aging, weakening physical frame. He looked as if he took personal responsibility for the fact that after a half-century of preaching the gospel to the whole world, that very same world was in a bigger mess than it was when he started. Pulling himself up to the podium, he got God's attention on behalf of the nation and then went right to the opening statement of his prayer: *"Oh God, we have sinned...."*

I was alone at the time, watching on TV, when the image of Billy Graham and the shock of this opening statement hit me like a slap in the face. The words seemed to stretch out over a millennium. They sounded oddly good; it was a relief to hear them. And following those words, I could almost hear a national heave of the breast—a public bloodletting. Alone at my TV that morning, I felt the guilty downward glance of a nation as Billy Graham publicly put his finger on the real problem.

"Oh God, we have sinned."

We've come up with many other names for sin that are more pleasant. Names that hardly hurt at all. We've worked hard to rid ourselves of the negative influence of words like *sin* and *hell* and *guilt* and *wrath*. Suddenly hearing the word *sin* on television, coming from the steps of the capitol, no less, with the whole world watching, was a shock to the system.

Billy Graham said the "S" word and got away with it. For one truthful instant, a nation bowed its head, heard the real truth from probably the only voice it still had any chance of trusting, and no one disputed the charge. Not one peep. Of course, the window of guilt he opened would later be closed, insulated by the curtain of rationalization it takes us all to make it through another day. But in that moment, on a bright, cold January morning, we all seemed to know he was right.

Inaugurations are usually times for more optimistic sentiments: blue sky, dreams, hopes, change, fresh blood, untried talent. Like opening day at a baseball game, everyone in the stands is filled with the hope that this just might be the year the home team wins it all. Right up until the first pitch, everyone's in first place. No balls, no outs, no errors, no mistaken calls. And then Billy Graham has to pray, *"Oh God, we have sinned,"* and pin us all to the wall.

Nicodemus brought himself up to the edge of the circle of torchlight. It flickered in his eyes. Like a cautious cat, he moved in and out of the circle of light, wanting to get closer, but afraid.

Suddenly a tear-stained face filled his vision as if out of nowhere.

"Aren't you. . . ?"

"Nicodemus." He finished it for the man. "I have followed from afar. I wanted to come closer, but I've been foolish and afraid. Now I am too late."

"No, you aren't. You are here," said John, newly named son of Mary. "Come."

John gently took Nicodemus's arm and guided him closer to the women who were still huddled near the cross. They were in shock, out of touch with everything, even grief. They sat quietly, stunned from staring too long at the impossible. Nicodemus had resisted John, but once he was in the light and in the company of the others, he broke into a thousand pieces inside and started to cry uncontrollably. Suddenly he was touched and held and surrounded by people he did not even know, and they all seemed thankful for a fresh supply of tears.

Nicodemus looked into the faces of people he would have judged hours earlier and wondered at what he saw in their eyes. These were unlearned peasants, but they seemed to know and understand this grief better than he.

Then he looked at the body of Jesus, and in the lifeless form on the cross he saw himself—a tired old self-righteous man, weary of justifications and the foolish arrogance that kept him from people. He saw the ugliness of his pride and the lies by which he tried to maintain his superiority. He saw it all and hated himself in that moment, and he wept bitterly, alternately abhorring and longing for the touch he was receiving from those around him.

"He spoke of you often," said John with his arm on Nicodemus's shoulder. "He said you were one of the few in your position who could see."

"He did?" Nicodemus raised his wet eyes and wiped them with the sleeve of his robe. "I didn't know myself . . . until now."

"What will you do?" Nicodemus asked after a long pause.

"Breathe in and breathe out," said John mechanically, his eyes fixed on the body of Jesus. Then he turned to Nicodemus and added, "If I can."

"I will help bury him," said Nicodemus. "Joseph of Arimathea is coming."

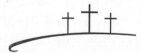

Something snapped inside me when Billy Graham said, *"Oh God, we have sinned."* Something snapped and spilled out all over. I had been found out. Oh yeah, *sin*. I remember that. It's been so long since I've heard about it. *Sin* is a word that seems to have dropped out of sight. It sounded like a word only someone as old as Billy Graham would remember.

I had lost track of it in places where I probably should have heard it—like on Christian radio, where callers meet a shrink on the air every day and receive reasons for their problems with gentle suggestions to soothe their guilty consciences. Or from the pulpit, where preachers have turned to more pressing issues lately such as abortion and homosexuals and condoms and prayer in schools. Or in Bible bookstores full of self-help books and Jesus junk.

But most of all, I had lost track of sin in my own life, coddling my ego and comforting myself with the failures and mistakes of others. The stockpile of ruined Christian lives and ministries is high right now; there are plenty of casualties to choose from, examples that could improve anyone's standing. Like a sanitary landfill of human destruction, this unhealthy place can provide hours of twisted comfort. "I know I'm running away from a problem I need to address, but look at that guy over here—he ran away from everything." Or, "Sure, I've gotten a little lazy with my thought life, but look at him! At least I kept my hands to myself."

Then Billy Graham had to go and say, *"Oh God, we have sinned."* And suddenly I'm in there with the best (and the worst) of them. He called our bluff. He lumped us all together. That's not fair. There are other words for these things—lapses in judgment, maybe, or poor choices, or less-than-desirable situations that trip us up from time to time. But to say we have *sinned* . . . well, that makes us all . . . *sinners.*

And I step around the untended responsibilities that are piled on and around my desk and get up to go for another cup of coffee, because this is getting to the part I knew I would have to get to if I wrote this book, and I think that now would be a good time for a break.

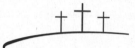

John had been right. Nicodemus *could* see. He had been working over the words of his midnight meeting with Jesus for over two years. He had figured out almost everything. He had figured out that Jesus was going to be lifted up like the snake in the desert. He had figured out that he was the final sacrifice. He compared Jesus' words with the words of Moses and the prophets and came up with what many of his colleagues refused to see: a suffering Savior who would come out of Bethlehem and die for the sins of the world. "He was wounded for our transgressions, bruised for our iniquities. . . ." Each new revelation had burst on his mind with blinding light.

Because he was not personally involved, in some ways he was able to look at the cross from the olive trees on the neighboring hillside and understand it in the scheme of things, perhaps even better than those who were huddled around it all afternoon. But what he did not know was what would happen to him once he got near enough to the cross to feel the splinters or touch the stiffening body. He was not prepared to see himself there, and he was definitely not prepared for what he finally did see.

Up until now he was dealing with Jesus and the prophets and the nation of Israel and the Gentiles in his mind—each part fitting like clues to a mystery that drew him closer and closer to the cross as if he were following a long shadow toward its source. But once he got there, right to it, standing right in front of God's intervention in human history, with all his knowledge and the new revelations he had gained, all he could see was Nicodemus and the sin of Nicodemus.

And all he could do was weep.

During the run of the pop psychology book, *I'm OK–You're OK,* a *New Yorker* cartoon pictured two men in business suits chatting with one another. In the background was a cross with someone hanging on it. The caption read, *If I'm okay, and you're okay, what's he doing up there?*

If a cartoon in a New York magazine can recognize it, it should be pretty obvious that sin is the only explanation as to why Jesus Christ came to earth. If he had been here just to show us how to live a fuller life as better people than when we started, he would certainly not have come to this sort of end. There would have been no reason for it. If there is no sin, there is no need for a cross. If he came for any other reason than to die this death on our behalf, then this death is a mockery.

But there is a thing called *sin* in the world, though you won't hear it talked about much anymore except from people like Billy Graham who have no other word for it. Sin is what is wrong.

Sin is what prevents even the most well-meaning of us from completely conquering the evil in our hearts. We may climb the highest mountain and yet descend to the lowest form of greed. We may find a cure for AIDS and yet be powerless against the bigotry, prejudice, and self-righteousness that festers in the hearts of gays and straights alike. We may give much of what we have to feed the poor but not be able to come up with even a morsel for the hunger in our own souls. We are a study in contrasts. We all ate of the fruit. We are filled with the knowledge of both good and evil at the same time, and we cannot always choose correctly. Something went wrong. The cross tells us that. If something hadn't gone wrong, we wouldn't need a cross.

Sin: a transgression of the law of God, Webster says. But sin is more than that. Sin is not only the act I did; it's the motivation that made me do what I did. Sin is both the nature and the deed. To a point, I can do something about the deed. I can compare my deeds to everyone else's deeds and arrange them to produce satisfactory results. I can fiddle with the law a bit to adjust it to the deed, but something keeps cropping up. Something deep inside me is the source of the deed like bad water that resists all attempts at purification.

Jesus said that it wasn't what goes into people that defiles them, but what comes out. "For from within, out of men's hearts, come evil thoughts, sexual immorality, theft, murder, adultery, greed, malice, deceit, lewdness, envy, slander, arrogance and folly. All these evils come from inside" (Mark 7:21–23). And if all these things come from inside, then they were there in the first place. That's the point. It's not bad influence; it's a bad beginning. There's something fundamentally wrong inside—something fighting against the right thing to do. And though we know this is true, we prefer to surround ourselves with those who would give us a better report.

To be sure, there are better reports to be found. Everywhere. In fact, we are hard pressed to find much mention of sin anywhere. There are plenty of pictures of Jesus dying and stretching out his arms for us and loving us on the cross (a stupid kind of love, indeed, without sin). But there's not much about sin itself. And if sin isn't real, that does away with the need for a cross in the first place. Even the *New Yorker* cartoonist knew that. But no one else seems to have noticed. People still sell the poster showing Christ with his arms out, and crosses have never been more popular. What we have is a kind of warm nebulous memory of the cross—without the sin, without the point.

Preachers used to go around convicting people of sin before they did anything else. A Wesley or a Moody or a Sunday or a Graham rolled into town, and a lot of folks would start feeling uncomfortable. Suddenly, on a citywide level, there was someone pointing out the fact that people weren't right with God. Something was wrong, and that something was *sin*. Sin messed up people's lives, their marriages, and their world. But someone did something about it. He is Jesus Christ. And they could come to the tent, Jesus would get them right with God, and the evangelist would help get them into a good church somewhere.

Today there are plenty of people in church, but for different reasons. Lots of people are in church today because it's the cool place to be. Mauve carpets, contemporary music, charismatic preachers, great drama, practical, useful messages, and good marketing are the hallmarks of the contemporary church. Not exactly your standard picture of folks running down front to get right with God. In fact, it has been statistically shown that the trend toward big churches does not reflect a growth in the number of converts as much as it does a shift in the worshiping habits of churchgoers. People from smaller churches are simply switching to bigger ones because they prefer them.

It even took a "secular" doctor to ask the question that we could not get around to asking ourselves: *Whatever Became of Sin?*[1] Leave it to the world to catch us in the inconsistency of our own bad theology.

"If I'm okay and you're okay, what's he doing up there?"

I know a group of men in New Jersey who know why he was up there. He was up there because they screwed up, that's why. These men were all in an alcohol rehabilitation program at America's Keswick Camp in Whiting, New

[1] Karl A. Menninger, *Whatever Became of Sin?* (New York: Hawthorne Books, 1973).

Jersey. I met them when I was speaking at a singles weekend retreat at the camp. They were part of a program that has been in operation there for over a hundred years. It combines an alcohol recovery program with the operation of a Christian camp open to church groups of all denominations.

Fifty men at a time can enter the ninety-day program. While they sober up, they are assigned duties of cooking, cleaning, serving meals, scrubbing toilets, and generally maintaining the camp. They have their own program staffed with qualified counselors and are exposed to a constant flow of great speakers and Bible teachers who pass through the camp for the various conferences being held there. Few of these men enter this program as Christians; fewer still leave as non-Christians. Their recovery rate defies anything the state has ever heard of.

I've never been around a more grateful, humble group. These men know about sin. Not sin in general, but sin in the personal.

While I was there, I gave a concert to the whole camp, and these men were invited. And I observed a marked difference between the men and the singles group I was speaking to for the weekend. The men from the program leaned forward in their chairs the whole night, hanging on to every word. And when I pulled out an old Kris Kristofferson song of a desperate but grateful forgiven sinner, you would have thought I had just dug up their national anthem.

I've performed this song before for other groups, and when I got to the last verse, I did what I always do—I called out, "Sinners only on the chorus!" The reaction of the two groups was like night and day. The weekend visitors squirmed and snickered as if it was a clever way to get them to think about themselves in a certain light. The guys from the rehab program joined in as if to say: "Hey, that's us! Come on, guys, sing it out! This is our big chance!" And sing they did, with all their might.

I believe these groups had different reactions to that invitation because they saw themselves in relation to their sin in fundamentally different ways. The singles group saw themselves as good people who sin sometimes; the rehab guys saw themselves as sinners. And there is a world of difference between these two perspectives. If there is something fundamentally wrong with us, then the problem is not merely that we screw up once in a while, it's that we are screw-ups.

I've always had a tendency to think of myself as something other than a sinner. I come from a good family. I've known God all my life. I've never committed any really bad sins. I've even believed God is pretty lucky to have me on his team. I'm a gifted child. I'm going to do something big for God someday. I'm special.

But the truth of the matter is, I couldn't be good if I tried! When I sin, it is not John Fischer messing up a little bit; it is John Fischer being the sinner that he truly is. I don't need just a little help in this—*I need to be delivered from myself.* There is something fundamentally wrong with me.

"Help me, Jesus, *I know what I am*" (a line in the rehab group's favorite song) turns out to be the most important line in Kristofferson's song. As the *Pogo* cartoon says, "We have met the enemy and he is us."

The great apostle Paul said, "Christ Jesus came into the

world to save sinners—of whom I am the worst" (1 Timothy 1:15). This comes as a big surprise. It continues to surprise me every time I read it. He didn't even say, as I would have expected him to say, "of whom I *was* the worst." No, Paul describes himself as a present-tense worst-case sinner. And he knows this will never change; that's why he needs the cross as a daily reminder that his problem is himself.

"But for that very reason I was shown mercy so that in me, the worst of sinners, Christ Jesus might display his unlimited patience as an example for those who would believe on him and receive eternal life" (1 Timothy 1:16). In other words, knowing who I am, what God is doing in my life is nothing short of a daily miracle. *This good life you see me lead,*" Paul seems to be saying, *"goes against my natural grain. It's a statement of God's unlimited patience that a guy like me gets to be shown mercy. Believe me, all of you: I know what I am."*

My problem is me. Your problem is you. We need to be delivered from ourselves because we are all worst-case, present-tense sinners. As Paul says, "What a wretched man I am! Who will rescue me from this body of death?" (Romans 7:24).

Getting him down was the hardest part. Joseph, John, Nicodemus, and the remaining guards worked together to lift the cross out of its hole in the ground and lower it down. There was no need to be careful anymore, yet Mary, his mother, kept crying, "Careful! Careful!"

As soon as his hands and feet were free, Mary wrestled

her way through the men to Jesus and lifted the lifeless body in her arms, cradling it as a mother would a child. The men stepped back and left her alone with him.

Silent tears ran down her face as she lovingly stroked his sacred head now wounded and caked with blood. Nicodemus noticed how awkward his body looked in her lap—his arms hanging down uncomfortably, his legs open and bowed. For a long time she hugged him, her face next to his. Then she laid him down gently next to the cross and backed away.

Joseph and Nicodemus went to work wrapping the body. Nicodemus had brought with him a mixture of myrrh and aloes, in accordance with Jewish burial customs, which they spread over strips of linen as they wrapped.

The tomb of Joseph of Arimathea was in a nearby garden. When it came time to transport the body, Nicodemus insisted. No. He would not listen to any protests. All the way to Joseph's tomb, Nicodemus carried the body of death.

5

BLOTCHES ON A PAGE

MY SON AND I had been staring at it for almost half an hour. The description said we were supposed to see a picture of Christ in a robe, standing just to the right of a small clump of trees. All we could see, however, was a random assortment of black blotches on a white page. I remembered this same trick picture from a number of years ago. It used to be a popular T-shirt during the Jesus movement, showing the hidden nature of Christ and giving the wearer an opportunity to witness to any curious inquisitors.

Whatever spiritual insight I once had into this picture, however, was of little use to me anymore. Nothing was coming. It's very frustrating to look right at something and not see what you are supposed to be able to see.

We can look right at the cross and never see it. We can stare at it forever and see nothing more than a religious anachronism. So much about the cross is a mystery; so little of it runs on the same track as our minds. Rarely is the cross what anyone is looking for. In fact, the very power of the cross lies in its inexplicable nature.

"For Christ did not send me to baptize, but to preach

the gospel—not with words of human wisdom, lest the cross of Christ be emptied of its power" (1 Corinthians 1:17). In other words, Paul is saying that if the cross could be put in terms that were obvious to every person, it would have no power to save. Its power lies in the fact that it runs counter to human wisdom. It is never the obvious solution. People can stare at the cross for a long time—all their lives, for that matter—and never get it.

Finally, as I stood there with my son, staring at the picture, it came to me. My mind suddenly interpreted the blotches from a different point of reference, and with a rush of recognition, the figure of Christ literally popped into view. But my son was not so fortunate, and my success served only to heighten his frustration. I even outlined the robe, the beard, and the clump of trees for him, but he still couldn't see it. He was about ready to tear his hair out when my wife walked by, glanced at the picture, and wanted to know why we had been staring at that picture of Christ for so long.

We do a disservice to the cross and the gospel when we try and explain it or make it obvious to everyone. If it could be understood by human wisdom, it would cease to be what it is. The cross is one thing we don't want to simplify. Its meaning is not going to pop into place for everyone. Nor is it up to us to make it make sense.

Christians need to learn to resist the temptation to make the gospel seem obvious. This has been our problem for the past twenty-five years. We need to learn to be more comfortable with ambiguity. When we present the gospel to our culture, we are, in many ways, asking them to stare at a bunch of blotches on a page. We are always trying to get everyone to see what we see, but this is impossible. The message of the cross is purposely countercultural; its meaning cannot be grasped by everyone, but only by those to whom God chooses to reveal it. Our job is not to get people to believe, but to hold up the picture. God's job is to make the image pop into place. When we try to make everybody see, we are messing with God's part. We will never do this as well as he does.

Even in the story, the way the Bible tells it, a lot of ambiguity remains. The Bible does not fill in all the blanks. In some ways, the Bible is nothing but random blotches on a page. One of the greatest temptations of Bible study is to try to "get it all down." Give it up. We will never get it all. You don't teach truth by outlining the picture for everyone and making them feel dumb for not seeing it. No, you paint it the way it is in all its apparent incongruity. You hold up the picture with blotches on the page and stay out of God's way. He's the one who will bring it into focus.

It was like this with the parables. Jesus would tell a story, and the people would hear it and scratch their heads. Later he would explain it privately to his disciples, and some of them still wouldn't get it. "The knowledge of the secrets of the kingdom of heaven has been given to you, but not to them," Jesus said when they asked him why he spoke in parables. "Whoever has will be given more ... whoever does not have, even what he has will be taken from him" (Matthew 13:11–12).

Jesus was always careful with the truth. He guarded it constantly. He never made it easy to get to; that would have been like casting pearls before swine or giving sacred things to dogs. When a person had a revelation about Jesus, he warned the individual not to tell anyone, and when people got the point, they were blessed because they saw it, as if it wasn't a common occurrence.

Well, it wasn't; Jesus made sure of it. He was always putting the truth just beyond their reach. Luke says the people "hung on his words," and I believe that was because Christ kept them hanging. He never filled in all the blanks for them; he never gave the ending away. He always kept them guessing—kept them staring at a bunch of blotches on a page, knowing the picture would pop into place for some and not for others.

Jesus shrouded the truth because he trusted in two things: the power of the Father in bringing people to himself ("no one can come to the Father except the Father draw him"), and the intelligence and desire of the individual to know truth and come after it.

This should come as no surprise to us. Coming to know about God has always been a two-way street. Truth is something God has always made us work for. God has never been fond of easy access to truth. He's hidden his truth in the heavens and the mountains and the trees of the field, and in the words of the prophets, crazy men and women rejected by the masses, recognized by the few. He has always painted his truth in such a way that you can stare at it for hours and never see it. But, oh, the glory when you do, when it finally pops into place and his truth is all you can see, everywhere! This is the way the master artist does his work.

Nowhere is the hidden work of God more evident than in God's display of Christ on the cross. Everything about Jesus dying there is not what it appears to be. The cross looks powerless, yet it is the power of God unto salvation to all who believe. The cross is the means by which Christ has overcome all other powers, including Satan: "Since the children have flesh and blood, he too [Christ] shared in their humanity so that by his death he might destroy him who holds the power to death—that is, the devil—and free those who all their lives were held in slavery by their fear of death" (Hebrews 2:14–15).

What appears to be a symbol of defeat is actually a symbol of triumph. The cross was designed to make a public spectacle of a criminal. Like hangings and beheadings and other forms of public executions that have been used throughout history, the cross was intended to be a deterrent to crime for any other would-be criminals who might be entertaining thoughts of similar lawlessness. But with Christ, the normal significance was reversed. You don't see this until the picture pops into place. "And having disarmed the powers and authorities, he made a public spectacle of them, triumphing over them by the cross" (Colossians 2:15).

This is the sting of the cross. At first it looks as if Christ is the one who is being made a spectacle of, and then all of a sudden we realize it is us. You and I are the criminals. This was what Nicodemus discovered. It is also what the rulers and authorities of darkness found out, much too late to do anything about it. The evil smile must have vanished from their faces when they discovered that the cross, their moment of triumph, was actually their undoing. They threw their worst at him, and it came back on them. He triumphed over them not by fighting with them or resisting them, but by taking the evil upon himself and then putting it away, ultimately forever, by virtue of his resurrection.

God, the master Creator, the genius behind this strange and glorious plan, is the one who holds us in suspense. This is God's drama being worked out here on the earth, and we are all watching, trying to make sense of the picture.

People who appreciate good art, music, or writing know the joy of finally seeing truth revealed. They also are familiar with the frustration that precedes such a revelation, and they are willing to wait. They even love being tricked, as long as the true reward for their patience is coming. Good artists know how to conceal the real treasure of their work and let the observers come to their own conclusions. The result is a mutual interaction of artist and audience, one of respect and honor. The audience respects the artist's ability to weave the truth into a new brocade, and the artist is counting on the audience's ability to unravel it. To lay it out for everyone, as if they were dumb for not seeing it, is nothing short of an insult.

Unfortunately, Christians have done major damage in the world by insulting people in this way. Preachers preach with huge chips on their shoulders, chiding people who don't see it. They are forever insulting the intelligence of the average unbeliever. They pride themselves in what they see. They are like the Pharisees who stand at the gate of the kingdom and keep the riffraff out.

Well, heaven is going to be made up of riffraff—all

those folks for whom the picture popped into place one dark night alone in a hotel room or kneeling in some church or lying in a bed with tears running down the sides of their faces. They'll all have their own stories to tell of the actual moment the picture first came into focus. It caught them all by surprise. No one was shouting at them. No one was insulting them. No, God himself was drawing them, and when he finally let them see, it was all they could see.

It's like that, you know. Once you see it, you see it every time. It's all you can see, until you can't believe that what you are looking at—this beautiful picture of Christ in a robe, standing just to the right of a small clump of trees—was once nothing but a bunch of blotches on a page.

"I see it! I see it! Oh my gosh!" It was my son, the next day, finally seeing the figure of Christ emerge from the page when he pulled the picture out for one more look. I understood just how he felt.

6

NO RAM FOR GOD

THE MAN TOOK THE WOOD for the burnt offering and placed it on his son's back. He himself carried the knife and a basket of coals for the fire.

"Stay here with the donkey while the boy and I go over there," he said to his two servants, pointing to the mountain that rose in the distance. "We will worship, and then we will come back to you."

Together father and son set out up the trail that led up to the mountain called Moriah. They had traveled three days to get here, and now the man knew this was the place. For the longest time the only sound was the stack of wood on the boy's back straining against the leather thongs that held it—that and the heavy breathing of the father. The boy kept up a steady pace, stopping occasionally to wait for his father to catch up. It was shaping up to be a fine autumn day, and the crisp morning air was perfect for hiking.

They switched back up a steeper rocky portion of the trail that forced them closer together—almost on top of each other. "Father," the lad said.

"Yes, my son?"

"The fire and the wood are here. . . ." His words came in the gaps of his measured breathing. "But where is the lamb . . . for the burnt offering?"

The old man did not reply immediately. For the last three days, his mind had been filled with happy pictures of his son—all the way back to his and Sarah's reaction to God's announcement that they would have this son. They had both laughed, and yet that laughter of disbelief and sarcasm had turned into a joyous laughter of such complete and utter surprise. *So this was how he was going to do it. We should have known all along that it would have to be something utterly impossible to figure out.*

All they could do was laugh. All the years of worry, of doubt, of manipulation, of trying to hold on to a shred of hope, losing that hope with Sarah's passing years—then suddenly there it was, right in front of them. As simple as a promise from a God who could do the impossible.

And now that same God was asking for yet another impossibility. Why not? It had been done before. The boy he loved, with the sacrificial wood on his back, swaying and bouncing up Mount Moriah in front of him, was a miracle. God was capable of anything. It had taken the father every bit of all three days to get to it, but now he was ready.

It was all from the same God: the child, the promise through the child, the unreasonable command for a most unreasonable human sacrifice. If that same God, for reasons of his own, now wanted the child back, then there was no other conclusion but to assume he must be able to raise him from the dead. This boy—this son whom he loved, who now carried the wood of his own funeral pyre—was the one in whom the promise lived. God had made that clear. This son; no other. It was God's problem now, not his. He would obey.

He opened his mouth and said the only thing he could say to his trusting child. "God himself will provide the lamb for the burnt offering, my son."

When they reached the place, they built an altar. The boy brought large smooth stones one by one, and the father stacked them. They worked well into the afternoon until they had formed a large platform. All this time the father was quiet, and the boy wondered why.

After arranging the wood on the altar, the father turned to his son, put his hands on his shoulders, and looked into his eyes for the first time since they started building the altar.

"Trust me" was all he said.

Then he took the leather thongs that had been around the wood and started to wind them around the boy's arms and legs. The boy laughed when this began, thinking it was going to be a game. But he saw no playfulness on his father's face—only a marked determination that grew with intensity as he pulled the leather tight and began tying it off.

"Ow!" said the boy as his father pulled on the cords. "Father, what are you doing?"

The boy's father made no reply but worked even faster with his fingers as if he were afraid something would pull him away from his purpose. He remained intent on his work, refusing to cast even a glance in his son's face.

Then the father lifted his bewildered child in his arms. He turned first to face the plains toward their home and then to the altar, where he placed the boy on the wood. A look of horror flooded the boy's face, but he did not speak. The man quickly removed a long-handled knife from his belt and raised it high over his son.

"Father!" cried the boy.

"Abraham!" cried the heavens. "Abraham!"

"Here I am," the man replied, the knife shaking in his hand against the clear blue sky.

"Do not lay a hand on the boy. Do not do anything to him. Now I know that you fear God, because you have not withheld from me your son, your only son."

And in the thicket they found a ram.

There was a ram for Abraham, but where was the ram for God? God's Son was on a cross. Nailed to it. But there was no ram in the thicket this time. No other provision. This was it. This was the only Son God had, and this was what all the bloody sacrifices were all about. God saw to it that for other fathers there was a substitute. But when his time came, there was none. His Son was the Lamb, the ram caught in the thicket for you and for me.

There was no substitute for the substitute. Jesus had cried out to his Father the night before; he had pleaded for him to figure out another way to do this. But there was none. Abraham had the benefit of God standing over him ready to provide a ram at the proper time. God, in the same situation, had no God. He had only himself, and he had no choice but to plunge the knife and turn away. This was what had to be. He had already decided this before time began.

"My God, why? Why have you forsaken me?"

Jesus did not fare as well as Isaac. Isaac was never forsaken. Confused for a moment, but not forsaken. Jesus was forsaken. Abandoned. Cut off. Left alone among men to die a slow, painful, and humiliating death. There was no ram; he was the ram caught in the thicket of our sin.

Sacrifice is hard for me to understand. Sometimes I think that if I lived in another place or another time, it might be easier. If I lived in a rural setting, perhaps, where animals and blood and the life and death of many creatures are more common occurrences, maybe then I could grasp this concept. In my culture and time, people hardly ever witness a death. People die quietly and alone in hospitals behind walls and curtains, and their blood drains into a plastic bag as they go pale.

But it is not only my culture that separates me from sacrifice. It is my religion as well (or lack of it). For I am a Gentile. I have no history of sacrifice. I never went with my father to sacrifice anything on a mountain and worship God. I read about sacrifice in the Scriptures; I can understand blood atonement for sin intellectually, but I have no experience in real life to attach it to. Not even a liturgy.

Abraham was steeped in this tradition. Blood sacrifice was a part of pagan religions surrounding him. Among them, human sacrifice was more common. This request from God was not made any easier by Abraham's traditions, but at least such a request was not nearly so odd to him as it would be if God were to ask it of me today.

Why was someone's death required? Why blood? Sometimes I can only stare at the cross and wonder, but it helps that the cross is in the middle of the room and not on a back wall. The need of a sacrifice for sin is much more important than I usually make it. I can't just sin and say I'm sorry. There's so much more to it.

Ours is a holy God. He makes impossible demands on us. He has a place in heaven prepared for us, but we're going to have to be different people than we are now if we are going to occupy it. Would you want to live with yourself for eternity the way you are now? In my opinion, *that* would be hell! There are no second chances in heaven. No New Year's resolutions. The sin problem in our lives has to be completely eradicated in order for God's plan to work. Death is the only way out. Death, over and over again, as in the case of the sacrifices of the Hebrews, or death once and for all—God's own Son, the final Lamb without blemish, an acceptable sacrificial death to pay the penalty of the sins of the world.

The essential sacrifice of Christ is a concept that has to come by faith. It is important to me because it is important to God. I will probably never understand it the way he does, but that does not matter. God didn't ask me to understand it. He only asked me to believe—to look upon him who was slain and believe.

There is one thing I do understand, however. I have a son about Isaac's age. I can think of nothing in this world that would be harder for me than to do what God asked of Abraham. Then I think of how God spared Abraham and went through it himself . . . on my behalf, and yours. Suddenly that love we talk and sing about becomes real—as real as Abraham's ram, waiting in the thicket to die.

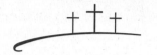

The trip down the mountain was full of laughter. They had nothing to carry but the empty basket, the leather thongs that once bound Isaac, and the knife that slit the throat of a ram.

Sometimes the boy would skip with glee and then turn back, glorying in his youthful energy, to run uphill to his father. Three times he ran ahead and circled back off the trail to hide behind a rock. Then he would jump out right in front of the approaching footsteps, and his father would leap back, gasping in surprise.

It worked every time—or at least, like every good father should, Abraham acted like it did.

Halfway down, they stopped to rest and enjoy part of a sweet onion and some dried meat they had brought for the trip. The father had wine in a wineskin around his neck and a roll left over from the morning that he broke and shared with the boy.

"Father?"

"Yes, son."

"Did you know there was going to be a ram?"

"No."

"What would you have done if there wasn't?"

"I would have obeyed God."

They ate for a while in silence. Both shuddered at the thoughts that were in their minds as a warm afternoon breeze blew through the pines and junipers that dotted the hillside.

"Poor ram!" said the boy, teasing.

"Ah," said the father, "never have I seen a lovelier ram!"

The truly wonderful thing to know is that I am the boy in this story. This is no longer a story of Abraham and Isaac. This is God and me. I am the one who was spared. I was bound and laid on the wood, but there was for me a ram in the thicket. I get to walk back down the mountain with my Father, with a lighter load, and with this death behind us. And when we laugh, it is deep and with great relief.

7

MY SIN

SIN IS NOT SUCH A BAD WORD after all. We have an unnecessary aversion to it. There is a sense in which *sin* should be a favored word in any believer's vocabulary—even something to be cherished. When Billy Graham prayed, *"Oh God, we have sinned,"* a bell rang in the tower of truth, and some people welcomed it.

Sin, in its best sense, is the problem properly diagnosed, and when the diagnosis is accepted, we feel a certain amount of comfort. Most people know what it is like to have the physical symptoms of a disease identified. This can be as serious as the discovery of a brain tumor that justifies weeks of unexplained headaches, or something as common as a child's earache that is shown to be the result of a discernible infection, treatable with simple antibiotics.

It can actually be a relief to find out there is something wrong with you when you have been shadowboxing at various symptoms for too long. Sometimes people even try to get you to believe there isn't anything wrong when you know good and well there is, like the mother who knows that the persistent crying of her infant is more than just the cutting of new teeth. The greatest relief, of course, is to find out that the problem is curable, but even in cases where it is not, such as with cancer or AIDS, people commonly report finding some resolution at least in meeting the enemy and being able to put a name and a face to the ugly truth.

So it is with sin. We do not reconcile ourselves easily to the presence of sin in our lives. It takes a conversion process. The natural thing is to think that we can control our instincts and overcome our evil tendencies. We are rational beings. By educating ourselves we can slowly evolve into something better. But as we go on, we find that our best intentions are constantly being tripped up by something we fail to take into consideration. Something is upsetting all our calculations. That something is the presence of a sin nature. And when we admit our sin, we put a name and a face to what we have known was wrong all along.

Herein lies the joy of our salvation. It is a thorough and complete salvation, because it goes all the way to the bottom of ourselves. Any solution to a predicament that does not sufficiently acknowledge the problem will be an inadequate one. The cross attacks the real problem right up front. There is comfort in this, and a certain relief.

Sin has an antidote. Something can be done. Something has already been done to take care of it. The cross is the cure that enables us to face and even embrace our sin. When the test for an incurable disease shows positive, even though the initial reaction may be denial, at some point the patient must accept the presence of the deadly thing in order to deal with it. How much more should I be able to face and admit my sin—even welcome it—when I know that something has already been done to take care of it.

The hymn writer spoke of such an understanding of sin when he wrote,

> My sin—oh the bliss of this glorious thought—
> My sin, not in part, but the whole,
> Is nailed to the cross, and I bear it no more:
> Praise the Lord, Praise the Lord, O my soul![1]
> —Horatio G. Spafford

In this hymn, the joyous statement "Oh the bliss of this glorious thought" is purposely sandwiched between two acknowledgments of "my sin." The glorious thought is about what happened to that sin, but the light of that glory shines back on the sin itself, as if it, too, were a part of the glorious thought. And to the extent that my sin readies me for salvation, qualifies me to accept it, then the sin, too, is swallowed up in glory. If I did not know sin, I would not now know my forgiveness. I would wander endlessly, harassed by symptoms of a disease I could never locate or identify, hounded by the harmful thoughts and deeds I could never admit.

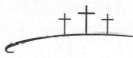

Simon was a good man. Simon was a careful man. It was important to him what God thought. That's why he had become a Pharisee: to get to the bottom of it. He liked the way the law spelled out things. There was a security in

[1]Horatio G. Spafford (1828–1888), "It Is Well With My Soul."

knowing exactly what God required of him and a personal satisfaction in being able to pull it off. He tried hard not to condemn people who were not Pharisees: publicans and sinners, women of the streets, tax collectors, and common folk. He tried to believe they were helpless in their ignorance, and yet he couldn't always talk himself out of the predisposition to judge. He had done something constructive with his life after all. Why couldn't they?

Simon was well aware, too, of the excesses of his own religious practices and beliefs. Some days he didn't like being a Pharisee—days when the zealous attendance to every detail of the law seemed to smother a deeper, more fundamental compassion for people that occasionally flickered in his soul like a dying ember. For this reason, he thought himself more balanced than most of his fanatical cohorts. Especially those who advocated snuffing out the life of some new would-be Messiah, the one some were calling (God forbid) "the Christ." True, the man was guilty of blasphemy if he had called himself this, but as far as Simon was concerned, there was no harm done. Another day, another self-proclaimed savior of the common folk. Let them comfort themselves with this at least.

Besides, something about this alleged Messiah was different than the rest. His blasphemy aside (and there was some question as to whether he had made the libelous claims himself or whether they were thrust upon him by his followers), there was something about this upstart country rabbi that fanned the ember in Simon's soul. He actually found himself enjoying hearing this Jesus talk. Of course he didn't tell anybody this—he had hardly even admitted it to himself. But when the young rabbi spoke, well . . . it was like a fresh wind blowing dead flesh off the bones of ortho-doxy and rattling the whole skeleton as if to prepare it for Ezekiel's miracle all over again.

That wind, and his own flickering ember, must have driven him to invite the man to his house for dinner. That, and his ongoing reputation among his Pharisee friends as a moderate. Simon took pride in being open-minded.

"Why not have the man over?" he said, lavishing his generous spirit on himself and his friends. "Let's find out for ourselves what he has to say."

It is truly an apt picture of modern man—trying to be-lieve there is nothing wrong, while knowing deep inside that there is. This is certainly the theme of countless novels, plays, and films. The Woody Allen films I have seen, for in-stance, present a constant stream of inner psychological di-alogue between people and their vague, nagging sense of guilt. It matters not whether the guilt is real or imagined. The fact that the conversation takes place—and we all rec-ognize it—is proof itself of the universality of the dilemma.

This inner dialogue of accusation and defense is a con-stant Allen theme that stretches across movie after movie, from therapist to therapist. It is largely responsible for what makes his films seem so real. But they are only marginally popular, because they take us too close to reality to provide any comfort. We have to meet ourselves on the screen too realistically, without any hope of solution or absolution. We just go on with these inconsistencies and these accusing voices in our heads and somehow scrape together, from the remnants of our mistakes, some semblance of meaning in life. The only comfort available in these films is to be able to laugh at yourself and go on, comforted at least by relief of not being the only one whose life is like this.

Good art is always true to this dilemma. It meets the problem head-on and offers few solutions. Good art stops short of calling the problem sin, but that is only because sin is a moral/spiritual term with which the world is uncomfortable. Good art may not name it, but it shows us the problem and often makes us stare at it too long for comfort. Good gospel, on the other hand, names the problem and solves it all at the same time.

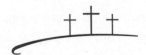

The four Pharisees Simon invited to dinner that night were used to the strange guests their friend often brought home. The list included a Roman soldier, a sorcerer, an idol maker, and a man who had been allegedly healed of a shriveled hand by their current guest of honor—on the Sabbath, no less.

But Simon didn't treat the rabbi like a guest of honor. He avoided the customary foot washing, anointing with oil, and kiss of greeting that washed the pains of the road from an honored traveler and prepared him to recline at table.

Simon's friends made no note of this oversight. They were used to treating people with inequity. But Jesus noticed. He and the three friends who accompanied him reclined at this particular table feeling dirty from the road and unkissed—unwelcomed strangers at a table to which they thought they had been invited.

Simon didn't mean to be rude. This was the way it was done. Honor was only bestowed upon one of like kind. Perhaps if his robed friends had not been with him and Simon had been acting from his heart—that place where the ember was trying to glow—he might have acted differently. But to invite the man to his house *and* treat him like an equal would have been taking his moderation one step too far.

"How did *she* get in?" whispered one of Simon's friends. A woman of the streets had come in the door and headed straight for the feet of their dishonored guest.

"Followed *him* in, I suppose," said another under his breath. "They're all friends, you know."

Their guest was unaware of their conversation, or so it seemed. He was intent on the woman, who was weeping profusely at his feet, wetting them with her tears and wiping the salty, muddy mixture from his feet with her hair. The weary rabbi made no attempt to dissuade her. Indeed, he seemed to draw strength and honor from her indulgence. His whole being was open to receive and enjoy what this woman had brought him. For a moment, it was as if there were only the two of them in the room. All was quiet except for the woman's gentle sobbing.

Then in the faint candlelight, away from the table where the rabbi's legs were stretched out, Simon thought he saw her kissing his feet. Then his nose caught the marked fragrance of a perfume. Not the subtle essence of nobility, but the gaudiness of the street. This was the smell of someone with something to sell. This was the unmistakable brazen odor of a prostitute.

Most people when they think of sin, immediately think of condemnation. Black thoughts. Images of dark rooms and whispers. Red-faced authority figures. Punishment—even abuse. All the bad things you ever did as a child, and all the bad things that may have happened to you as a result, have a way of cropping up in the vicinity of the word *sin*. *Sin* conjures up images of going before the priest or the principal and telling the truth, or risking trying to get away with a lie. It usually means I've gotten caught and I'm going to have to appear before someone who has the power to convict me.

But what if sin is ultimately connected to forgiveness? What if the person I have to go before has already obtained forgiveness on my behalf? Wouldn't that change the way I looked at sin? What if God, after all, isn't my third grade teacher who screamed at me, or the father who abused me, or the priest who condemned me? What if God is not only the judge, but the one who has obtained, at great personal cost, a pardon on my behalf?

What if, in fact, accepting this pardon was the only way I could ever get to know this side of him? Wouldn't sin take on a different meaning in my life at that point? If admitting my sin were the only way to get forgiven, wouldn't my sin suddenly become a valuable possession to me—a sort of ticket to my freedom?

This is indeed the bliss of which the hymn writer spoke. *"My sin—oh the bliss of this glorious thought..."* My sin has brought me to the cross; the cross has brought me to Christ; Christ has paid for my salvation; my salvation has made me right with God. The thing that was my undoing has become my only hope.

But there is a catch. This is a personal process that involves a personal knowledge of sin. It cannot be handled in the abstract. The sin spoken of here is not generic. It is personal sin—*my* sin. How ironic that a real relationship with God begins here. Regardless of my knowledge of biblical truth, my years of service for God, or my religious devotion to study and piety, a relationship with God cannot go any further than the realization I have of myself as a sinner—including, of course, the knowledge of those sins at which I am an expert. These things have real names like lying, cheating, coveting, lusting, being a lover of self versus a lover of God.

Indeed, this issue of personal sin is one of the greatest problems a person can face—especially if he or she has grown up in the church.

I can remember as a child trying to grapple with some dark feeling I was supposed to have when the pastor talked about sin, because that's what everyone around me seemed to be doing. Pictures of Jesus hanging on a cross flooded my mind, but I had no means of understanding them. I think in those moments I was much more sorry for him than I ever was for myself. I was too young to have reconciled myself to the sin in my life. There was no bliss in the cross for me—only a kind of dark foreboding I did not understand. Jesus died this horrible death for me there. But why? Until I understand that my own personal sin is the "why" of the cross, the cross and God himself will remain distant.

I have visited churches in New England that once had "box seats" for the most prominent members, complete with a brass name marker on the door to the pew. And I wondered how a person who was aware of sin and the need for forgiveness could take such a position.

Labels on pews are not as common today. But a position in the choir, a permanent nametag as a server or an usher, or a place of power in the politics of the church can result in a similar false security, distancing us from our own personal knowledge of sin. And thus we struggle when the Communion plate is passed, wondering what this was all for and feeling sorry for Jesus instead of feeling sorry for our own sins that caused his death.

The value of the cross is directly proportionate to my awareness of my own sin. The minute I fail to see my own sin, the cross loses its meaning. As soon as my problems can be explained on some basis other than sin, then the cross becomes superfluous. I may try to have it stir my heart, but it has no real connection to me. My sin, and nothing else, will make me cling to this hard, ugly beam of wood. As difficult as the cross is to understand, only my sin will give it any meaning at all.

It seems likely to me that the primary deficiency Christianity faces in this beginning of the twenty-first century is not a lack of understanding about the cross or the gospel. What's missing is the knowledge of sin.

Crosses adorn our churches and hang around the necks of paupers and movie stars alike. Passion plays always demand attention, and theaters everywhere still find success with *Jesus Christ Superstar* and *Godspell*. Good Friday is a half-day off for most businesses, and the average American attends church on Easter weekend more than any other time in the year.

How with all the television and radio preaching of the born-again movement could the true meaning of the cross escape the average person? It is probably because no one is telling people that it is *their own sins* that are nailed there.

Surely this man cannot be so naïve, thought Simon as he smelled the heavy aroma of a prostitute's perfume coming from Jesus' feet.

But before Simon's thought was fully formed, the young rabbi turned and looked him in the eye. "Simon," he said, as the woman continued caressing his feet, "I have something to tell you."

"Tell me, Rabbi," Simon responded. His four ceremonially robed guests all turned to him in surprise when he addressed the peasant as *teacher*.

"Two men owed money to a certain creditor. One owed him five hundred dollars, and the other fifty. Neither of them had the money to pay him back, so he canceled both debts. Now, which of them will love him more?"

Simon felt as if he were about to be suckered, but he went along for the point. "I suppose the one who had the bigger debt canceled."

"You have judged correctly," Jesus said. Simon could

hardly feel proud about being applauded for this obviously simple judgment. In front of his friends, in fact, he felt a little ridiculous. But the young rabbi ignored the quivering pride of his host, turned toward the woman, and continued speaking to Simon while his eyes remained on her. She carried on with her strange offering, too humble and lowly in her intent to return his gaze. His feet were all of Jesus that she wanted, as if tending to them would somehow make her forget everything about her life that she hated.

"Do you see this woman?"

Could he *see* her? Of course he could see her—and smell her. He couldn't get away from her!

"I came into your house. You did not give me any water for my feet, but she wet my feet with her tears and wiped them with her hair."

He gestured and kept talking to Simon as if he were addressing the woman.

"You did not give me a kiss, but this woman, from the time I entered, has not stopped kissing my feet."

Simon was mesmerized; the other four Pharisees were aghast.

"You did not put oil on my head, but she has poured perfume on my feet. Therefore I tell you, her many sins have been forgiven—for she loved much."

At this the young rabbi finally turned his gaze from the woman and looked directly at Simon with eyes that blew away his dead flesh and rattled his bones. "But he who has been forgiven little . . . loves little."

The reason *sin* is such a bad word to so many people is that they have not heard the whole story from those who have been forgiven. When the preacher preaches the gospel, it's more likely *your sin* that we hear about, or quite possibly *humanity's sin* or *sin* in general—a sort of generic gospel with a black and white label on it. Rarely in my lifetime have I heard a preacher say the words: *my sin*. Rarely indeed have I said them.

Only those who have seen the cross, have seen their sin nailed there, and have truly received the faith to believe their forgiveness know the bliss. They can even go as far as to cherish their sin and the hard, splintery cross on which the Savior bore it, because through it they have received their most valuable possession: absolution from sin. Only then is *sin* not such a bad word.

Deep down inside, we long for God to blow the whistle on the whole game. Deep down inside, we want the truth, and when it finally hits home, it hits with incredible fierceness. It's the only way this will work. We are—every one of us—completely, utterly despicable sinners who are completely, utterly, and wonderfully saved. We gather around the same table, separated by society yet joined by God— Pharisee and sinner, weak and strong, beautiful and ugly, straight and gay, intelligent and ignorant alike, holding out our hands for the blessed forgiveness. There is no division here. No CASUAL SINNERS over here, or NICE PEOPLE SINNERS over there, or REALLY BAD SINNERS down there and to the left. We are all equally guilty, so we can all be equally and gloriously saved.

"Wait a minute," I can hear someone say. *"I agree we all*

*deserve death and separation from God and all, but is John Doe
really as bad as Hitler?"*

How else does this work? Are some separated further
from God than others? Will some be on the near side of
hell versus the far side? Or perhaps there are varying Fahr-
enheit settings comparable to the degree of the crime, and
Hitler has a special place reserved just for him in the boiler
room.

Some people may live out their sin to a fuller degree
than others. A dedicated, lifetime sinner is going to be more
in touch with sin than a moral Pharisee, but I don't see any
indication in the Scriptures of degrees of guilt. We have all
sinned and fallen short of the glory of God. Some are just
better at hiding it than others. There is no comfort to be
gained in being found less guilty than someone else if the
final decree is guilty, nonetheless.

More important, if grace saves me from less of a sin
than someone else, am I going to end up in a better neigh-
borhood in heaven? An ocean view condo, perhaps? (With
mauve carpets, of course!) Paul was the chief of sinners because he saw himself that way. He should have a major ar-
gument from all believers on this issue, for if we all saw
ourselves correctly, we would all say the same thing, even if
Hitler were in the room.

Christ told a humorous story about removing the telephone pole in my own eye so I can see clearly to deal with
the speck of dust that is in my sister's. He wasn't referring

to degrees of sin, but to degrees of *importance* of sin. My sin is like a telephone pole to me, compared to your speck of dust. Your sin is like a telephone pole to you, when you try to do something about the speck in my eye. It all has to do with perspective.

"But he who has been forgiven little . . . loves little." Not because he had little to be forgiven, but because he spent his whole life walking around with a telephone pole in his eye, bumping and crashing into everybody, and never saw it.

A hushed stillness filled the room. The woman was quiet now, leaning her head against his feet, holding on for dear life—for all the life she had ever known.

All Simon's friends could think about at that point was the audacity of this man to think he could forgive sins. All Simon could think about was his own guilt, the wind that was fanning the faint ember of his soul into a flame, and the wild impossibility never before entertained by his measuring, careful mind—that perhaps he, too, was a sinner who could be forgiven of his sins.

Simon discovered something that evening that changed his life because it altered his perspective. When Jesus accused him of loving less because he had less to be forgiven of, it wasn't, as he had first thought, because he was less of a sinner. He wrestled with this idea all night, after his guests were gone. For a while he entertained the thought of going out and committing some gross sin. Why not? He had always wanted to, and the perfume of the woman still hung in the house, taunting him.

Suddenly it hit him. He didn't need more sin in his life. He already had more than his fair share. His sin was that he had arranged his life in such a way so as not to see his sin. That in itself was his sin—the most hideous sin of all—to be full of sin and yet think yourself better than other sinners.

8

THE NEW POSSIBILITY

THE SUN ROSE THAT first Easter morning on an entirely different world than the one that had existed hours earlier. For most people, to be sure, it was the same. Birds twittered as they usually did in their predawn revelry. Lazy dogs barked at the sound of the first early risers. In his penthouse in downtown Jerusalem, Pilate rolled over in bed and moaned at the mockingbird making a racket on his veranda. He could feel his wife's stiffness next to him. He didn't even have to look to see her wide, sleepless eyes locked on a crack in the ceiling for fear of the dreams that might come back if she closed them.

In the nearby barracks, a soldier snored on in thick oblivion. Soon his comrades would wake up to wicked hangovers from the night before, a usual Sunday morning experience. Things were always quiet on the Jewish Sabbath, so Saturdays became party time for the Roman soldiers.

Out in the courtyard, roosters crowed, and Peter, curled up next to a stone wall, was sure he heard every last one of them. He hadn't been sleeping, either. All those great plans and dreams for himself and his nation had vanished with three denials and two rooster crows. Roosters had been rattling and cackling in his brain for two nights. They wouldn't let him sleep, and they wouldn't let him forget that look on the Savior's face that left him frozen in his betrayal.

On the edge of town, three women made their way quietly through abandoned narrow streets, clutching vials of sweet-smelling perfume. In the hazy light of early morning, they were headed for Joseph's garden, where the dead body of the man they once thought was the Son of God lay without proper respect. There had been no time on Friday to anoint the funeral wrappings, and such activity was forbidden on the Sabbath. Nicodemus and Joseph had done a credible job with limited time and little preparation, but it was barely adequate. The women had their own idea of how this needed to be done, and they were setting out to fulfill those requirements—as much for their own sake as for the sake of the custom.

Just when they started to wonder who might help them move the huge stone over the face of the tomb, they found, lo and behold, that the stone had already been moved away. The soldiers guarding it shifted on the ground in a deep, impenetrable sleep; the wrappings that should have been around the body lay limply on the rocky shelf inside. And an angelic being bright as lightning asked a question that would change them forever: *"Why do you seek the living among the dead?"*

There has never been, nor will there ever be, anything quite like the resurrection of Jesus Christ. It turned everything upside down, changed the rules, rewrote the book. You could stop the earth and start it spinning the other way, and the change wouldn't come close to this. There is nothing quite as show stopping as what the angel said to these women:

"Why do you seek the living among the dead?"

Why do you expect everything to be the way it was? Why do you think everything can be explained in the old terms of cause and effect? Why are you putting your faith in science—in the laws of nature and the decomposition of human cells? Why are you trying to explain everything in ways you can understand? Why are you holding those vials of perfume in your hands? If you're looking to anoint his feet like you did in the house of Simon, I'm sure you can find him somewhere around here. He can't be far. Then again, he could be halfway around the world, come to think of it, because nothing is the same anymore. Why do you go on living your life the way you always have? Why are you trying to live in a world without miracles? Why do you look to your own resources—your little vials of perfume—as if all you can do is anoint the body of a dead man who isn't going to be where you think he is? The man is no longer dead. Don't you get it? Didn't you hear him when he told you about this? Nothing is the same now. Nothing.

Faith always seems to break in on me like the angel at the Resurrection. Usually, if I'm not God-conscious, I am most likely struggling with the obvious. Maybe I'm trapped in some form of legalism—some old tape from my childhood. Or maybe I'm simply trying to figure out my situation without factoring in God—The Impossible. Whatever is keeping my world small and manageable is a little like these women clutching vials of perfume for anointing a dead body at the tomb of the missing Christ.

We probably shouldn't blame them. It's all we can do sometimes just to keep alive and manage our responsibilities. All we've had to work with up until Christ are dead things. Our own plans and formulas—our own resolve to make a difference that we know will fail not long after we make it. The hopes and dreams that we keep telling ourselves are going to come true, even though we know better. Dead things. The boring routine that we keep repeating every day with no thought to its ultimate purpose or goal. The futility that life has become, now that we have lived it long enough to doubt.

Wait a minute. Were these women even *seeking* the living? No. They were there to anoint the dead. They weren't even entertaining the possibility that they might encounter anything living that early in the morning—anything more than a few barking dogs and maybe a lonely rooster now and then. That's what was so incongruous about the question itself. They were seeking the dead, and the angel asked them why they were seeking the living among the dead. The angel pierced the negative darkness of their gloom with the shining fact of a new reality. The angel treated them as if they were aware of the new possibility that had broken in upon the world.

Faith is always like this. It comes complete with a new way of seeing things that always takes us by surprise. It catches us in our smallness. It was a different world they woke up to, and they didn't know it yet. They were seeking the right person, but in the wrong place.

It's no different today. We won't find Christ anywhere near the weak rationalizations of our flesh. He is miles away from our unbelief. He does not wait for us to come anoint the cherished graveclothes of our excuses and our guilt. He is not trapped with us in any routine. The cross will always be an important sign to us, but he is not on it.

HE IS ALIVE! He is out among the living. Out where the kingdom has come and lives are being changed. Out where hopes and dreams really come true for those who believe and are willing to count on him for their daily bread. Out where his mercy makes us able to forgive, his riches make us able to give, his acceptance makes us able to come out of hiding, his power makes us able to act—out where his life makes us able to live.

In some ways, every morning is not that different from that first Easter morning when the sun rose on a new possibility. Birds still twitter, dogs bark, soldiers brace themselves for the worst, executives wake up with hangovers, lonely wives worry about their dreams, and believers lament, as roosters crow, how they could deny to the world someone so important to their hearts . . . and yet, it is a profoundly different world, a world that has never been the same since Jesus Christ arose.

And the sun rises each morning, like a bright angelic being, calling out to each of us in our doubt, our insecurity, our fear, and our need: "Why are you seeking the living among the dead? I'm over here. I know what you thought, but it's not what you think. You're wandering around graveyards preparing to pay respects, and I'm dancing on the morning. I'm blazing in the sky. I'm shimmering on the water, and I'm shining in your eye. Wake up! Every morning is Easter morning, and I am the possibility you haven't thought of yet!"

PART II

"Our experts are dyeing daily."

From a sign on the front window
of a Chinese laundry

9

DEAD OR ALIVE

THE CROSS THAT punctuates the sanctuary of the Presbyterian church in Old Greenwich, Connecticut, stands like a silent sentinel over the spiritual life of its members. It is there at the first sign of morning light, and it is there as the last evening shadow surrenders to the darkness. It is not erected for evangelistic services or revival meetings and then taken down for the everyday life of the church. You are just as likely to bump into it while you are passing through the sanctuary on your way to a Tuesday night committee meeting as you are after sitting through a Sunday morning sermon.

This cross is off the wall. It has been pulled out of its place in history and firmly fixed in the present. It is not behind anyone; it is in the midst of the congregation and in the middle of everything. It is the permanent centerpiece of this church.

This commanding presence of the cross is unusual, especially for evangelical Christians. Catholics and Episcopalians are more familiar with crosses in the midst of everyday life and worship. Priests and bishops are always working in and around crosses. Crosses dangle from their necks or hang on banners draped over pulpits and tables. Crosses sit atop Communion articles and holy water bowls, and they bob up and down on the candlelighters of robed acolytes. But growing up as an independent, Bible-believing, fundamentalist Christian, I am accustomed to fairly bland, non-ornamental churches. Once every two months there would be crosses on the silver lids covering trays of thimble-sized Communion glasses, but other than the cross rendered in the round stained-glass window behind the choir loft, our view of the preacher was unencumbered by symbols.

This lack of symbolism is indicative of a certain theology as well. As an evangelical, I have become accustomed to viewing the cross primarily as the doorway to becoming a Christian. When I was growing up the cross was preached to people who were unsaved, remembered among believers as essential to salvation. But once you were a Christian, it pretty much faded back into the wall. The bulk of our time and attention was taken up with trying to be good Christians. The cross for us was part of a review course on salvation rather than a fundamental element of the life of faith. ("Okay, class, let's go over one more time how we got here. . . .") The cross was the way *in* more than the way *on*.

I now believe that our failure to deal with the cross as part of the daily walk of faith has contributed, among other things, to the legalistic manifestations common to my particular brand of Christianity. If the meaning and presence of the cross diminishes once we become Christians, than being a Christian is not much different than being a Pharisee. We are back to trying simply to be good people—or at least people who are better than most. All the cross accomplished was to get us in on the program. Once in, we are left to our own devices to come up with something that resembles what we think the finished product should be.

How quickly we forget. It took the sacrifice of Christ on the cross to get us to face our inability to meet the mark, but once saved, we want to put the cross behind us and go back to trying to meet the mark in our own way. We think somehow we're different people by nature when we get up off our knees than we were when we went down. True, we are by nature new creatures in Christ, but we are not, by that nature, rid of our body of sin. Paul's cry, "Who will rescue me from this body of death?" does not come once in a lifetime; it comes over and over again. The many references in Scripture to a believer's continual struggle with sin and the sin nature make it impossible to believe that this problem will somehow go away once a person is saved.[1]

The problems in our lives that brought us to our knees in the first place are not somehow magically resolved once we become Christians. As the women at the tomb found out, the possibilities are new, but in many ways we have remained the same. We still have our humanity, our doubts, and our sin to wrestle with. And if the struggle with human nature and with sin is a daily reality for the believer, then the cross must be a daily reality as well. Christ told us that following him meant carrying a cross every day. Yet we are apt to forget this part of the ministry of the cross in our lives.

The apostle Paul was well aware of our tendency to forget the cross after salvation. He warned the Galatians about

---

[1]See 1 John 1; Romans 8; 1 John 2; Galatians 5:16–18.

this very problem: "You foolish Galatians! Who has bewitched you? Before your very eyes Jesus Christ was clearly portrayed as crucified.... Are you so foolish? After beginning with the Spirit, are you now trying to attain your goal by human effort?" (Galatians 3:1, 5).

In other words, are we so foolish as to miss the connection between the cross of Christ and our present lives as Christians? "You saw him crucified," Paul said. "How can you go on living as if that crucifixion didn't make any difference in your life?" How, after being the cause of Christ's death on the cross, could we ever expect to perfect ourselves by human effort? Has salvation made us somehow immune to sin? Indeed not! We still reap what we sow (Galatians 6:7–8), and we are still in conflict between the Spirit in us and our sinful nature (Galatians 5:17). The cross will always be God's final statement on what he thinks about the best we can do.

The cross stands in the middle of things—a statement about our best efforts without it, and a guard against the notion of a casual grace. From childhood it was drummed into me that Christ's death on the cross covered all my sin—all the sins I have committed in the past and all the sins I will commit in the future. This may be true, but I wonder if too much liberty has been taken with this doctrine in the manipulation of our experience. What's to keep me from throwing this doctrinal blanket over all my present and future sins so I don't have to deal with them directly or specifically anymore? As long as my sins are covered, I can get along with my business, knowing that a little bit of sinning here and there isn't going to set off any alarms in the kingdom of God. All these sins have been taken care of, just as long as I don't take too much advantage of forgiveness. Habitual, intentional sin would be a problem, of course, but a little bit of sloppiness ... well, that's to be expected. We're only human, you know.

Intentionally or not, we fail to see that the cross is an indictment upon sin to both the saved and the unsaved alike. It says the same thing to everyone, and it says it all the time. There is not a separate gospel for those inside the church than there is for those outside. Nor is there a rugged, bloodstained cross before salvation and a more refined, softer one after. If it took the cross to save us, it's going to take nothing short of that same hard, splintery cross to get us to our goal.

But how does the cross get us along once we've started? The role of the cross in our salvation is one thing, but what role does it play after? How does the cross factor into the process of making us whole?

Simply put, the cross does for us what it did for Christ. It kills us.

We have found many ways around this truth. We have softer meanings by the truckload, ways of interpreting the cross that fall considerably short of a death. But it is useless to try to change the unavoidable. Where there is a cross there must also be a death. No one in history has ever half-died on a cross. If after a while a criminal was only half-dead, soldiers came by and broke his legs to speed up the process. They didn't take anyone down until he was dead.

In *Mere Christianity*, C. S. Lewis addressed this no-compromise death by having Christ speak to us in the following manner: "I have not come to torment your natural self, but to kill it. No half-measures are any good. I don't want to cut off a branch here and a branch there, I want to have the whole tree down."[2]

This idea of dying to self and "taking up your cross" is one of the hardest concepts in the Christian faith to understand. But it is hard not because it is complicated. It is hard because it is so difficult to accept. We try to complicate it precisely because we know intuitively what it means, and we do not like the idea. No one likes to die.

In an earlier draft of this chapter, I wrote a paragraph that does the very thing I have been warning about. It obscures the idea of dying to self. It sounds like an explanation when it is actually an evasion of the truth.

Here it is just as I wrote it:

> What is death but the absence of life? And what does the cross teach me in my daily life but that I cannot turn to any of my normal, natural resources for help. They are all dead to me. There is only one source of life in me now, and that is the Spirit of God. And I can count on the fact that God will arrange the events in my life so that I will be forced to discover this on a regular basis. I will always be frustrated when I turn to human effort alone to accomplish anything spiritual. It will be to me like beating on a dead horse.

I like this paragraph. I think it's pretty good, and it's even true in the sense that the Spirit of God is my only source of life. But as true as this statement might be, this is not what it means to die to self. It sounds like it is, but I switched the subject. It was a clever side step.

---

[2]C. S. Lewis, *Mere Christianity* (New York: MacMillan Publishing Co., 1976), 167.

Notice what I did. I took a very straightforward, direct concept—and put it in the abstract. I buried it so deeply in one paragraph that there is nothing I have to do about it. I even have God arranging the events in my life so I will have no choice but eventually to do the right thing.

This paragraph looks good on paper only. It does not demand anything of me. There is no confrontation here—no pain, no struggle, no death, just a nebulous idea. But death is not nebulous. Death is definite. Final. There are few things in life more certain than death.

The meaning of dying to self has to be something as obvious as the fact that . . . I die. I cease to be. I have to step over my body to get on with life. I am no longer the reason for my existence. I am no longer concerned with my own happiness. How can you be concerned with the happiness of someone who is dead? I am no more. I am no longer in the picture. I am no longer the center of my own little universe. I no longer arrange the world around myself. Go to the place where you used to find John Fischer, and you won't find him anymore. He's dead. The place is empty, and instead, you should encounter a shining being standing next to the door wanting to know why you are seeking the dead among the living.

At least this is the way it should be and the way it can be. Come to where you used to find me, and you should find Christ instead, living and caring for others at the expense of himself, like he always did. This is the way it should and could be for all of us who believe. If instead you find good old John Fischer still worrying and manipulating and measuring out his few spiritual coins and clinging to the coattails of his comfortable, debilitating fear, it is only because he doesn't want to die. He's clinging to the dead thing and telling himself it is more alive than Christ.

Dying to self has to mean I live for someone else. That is the whole point. Christ does not ask us to die just for the fun of it. Christ asks us to get rid of one life because he has a much better one in mind. Our old life is only capable of caring for its small little self. The new one is selfless, generous, broad in goodwill, and abundant with love and kindness. The new life loses itself in God and everyone else. The new life is like Christ when he gave up being God so he could be a servant. The new one is like Ebenezer Scrooge after the third ghost.

The clearest example I can think of in this regard is Paul's admonition to husbands to love their wives "just as Christ loved the church and gave himself up for her to make her holy" (Ephesians 5:25–26). My relationship with my wife shows me how little I know of this death. How have I "given myself up" for my wife, that she might be whole? Christ died so that we might live. Have I died so that my wife might live? More often than not, I have expected her to give herself up for me. Isn't that the norm? Wives lose everything to their husbands, while their husbands go on and do what they were going to do anyway. Jesus is asking me to do the opposite. If this relationship is a measure of the degree of my own grasp of this concept, then I know I have a long way to go.

Recently, in the middle of a transcontinental do-it-yourself move, I wrote the following reflection in my journal:

I'm presently stretched between two coasts, two mortgages, two addresses, three time zones, and an amount of perplexity that awakens me wide-eyed at that imperceptible time of night before you can legitimately call it morning—even early morning. Letters lie on my desk with yellow stickers attached: "NOTIFY SENDER OF NEW ADDRESS," and I would if it were possible to hit a moving target. My address for the last ten days has been a big yellow twenty-four-foot rental truck loaded with furniture and boxes rumbling across east/west interstates from coast to coast, seeking to do what I believe to be God's will.

Life was so much clearer when I was sitting eight feet up in a cab rolling down the highway. The purpose was obvious; the destination, mappable; and the rush—well, sometimes it was downright exhilarating. The last time I made this cross-country trip, I rented one of those orange-and-white trucks with "Adventure in Moving" on the back. And some adventure it turned out to be. The truck was a gutless wonder. I spent half a day going up steep inclines in the Rocky Mountains in second gear, at a top speed of eighteen miles an hour and holding.

Newer bright yellow rental trucks whizzed past me, and I vowed that if I ever made a long distance move again, I would rent something that didn't have "Adventure in Moving" on the back. This slow crawl was not quite the adventure I had in mind. Besides, ever since I was punished as a kid for playing with trucks in a sand-for-cement pile during backyard construction, I've always had an undying fantasy to be a trucker, and I can't qualify for even a shot at that experience if I can't keep up with the crowd.

So this time I rented myself a brand-spanking new, big yellow truck, picked up a black Harley Davidson cap at the first truck stop, punched in all the country music stations I could find, and rolled my six-wheeled, twenty-four-foot rig out of Massachusetts for the long trip to California. To my dismay, I found out that the yellow truck didn't have much more power than the orange-and-white one after all, except for one stretch of I–70 in Missouri where I must have had a tailwind and a level road. With my foot to the floor and my leg shaking like a scratching dog, I was right in there with the big boys—blinking my lights, passing and being passed, finding my spot in the long and winding trail of shiny diesel behemoths that stretched into the Missouri sunset.

It was a rush I will never forget, and for one moment, when six of us were locked in unison for about a five-mile stretch, I knew what it must feel like to fly in formation—to feel linked together by an invisible bond with the power of truly massive moving machines.

But something happened between Missouri and my desk here in southern California, and this isn't the first time it has happened. It's an awareness that life on stage or life on the road—like life on a full tank of gas on I–70—is only an illusion. That was I–70, and this is home. That was a temporary rush of success and clear purpose; this is human life as it actually is.

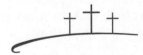

Daily life for a believer, as for anyone else, has highs and lows. The highs are different than what they used to be before one was saved. Worldly highs are often drug or alcohol induced—something foreign pumping through the veins that gives a euphoric sense of being above it all. For the believer, this high is induced by the Spirit of God. This is why Paul says, "Do not get drunk on wine, which leads to debauchery. Instead, be filled with the Spirit" (Ephesians 5:18).

The highs are similar; where they lead is not. One leads to debauchery, the other leads to song, to giving of thanks, and to living an empowered life. One manifests itself as lack of control, the other as self-control. This is the supreme elegance of life in the Spirit. It is available to all believers who reckon themselves dead to sin and alive to God, who depend not on their own resources, but on the Spirit's.

But that is not the way life always is, even for the most devout followers of Christ. Though I have been freed from this body of sin, it still sticks to my back like flypaper. I cannot rid myself of it. Though it is dead to me, I must personally deliver it to its grave, and I will not be free of it until I go in there myself and lay it to rest. And along the way, its old ways still trick me into thinking it is alive.

This is where the cross comes into the picture for the believer. Life as it actually is should have a cross in the middle of it all the time. I need to feel the cross and its splinters on a daily basis, lest I forget what Jesus Christ has done for me there and why. When I get up off my knees of confession, though I am forgiven, I do not cease to be a sinner. Like Nicodemus on his way to Joseph's tomb, I still carry around this body of death. I can still pamper it with perfume, even though in my heart of hearts I know I am foolishly seeking the living among the dead. The cross reminds me of reality and keeps bringing me back to my salvation—not that I need to be saved over and over again, but that I need to remember and stay close to the cross, for in it I see the dead thing for what it actually is.

The cross in the middle of my daily life triggers a life in the Spirit. It is a regular reminder. It faces me with my sin and reminds me of my forgiveness and the cost of my salvation. When I think about consciously sinning, I see Christ on the cross and I have to decide if I want to go ahead and contribute to his death one more time. I've actually been angry about this at times, wishing that picture would go away so I could resurrect the dead thing one more time without a conscience to bother me.

But the degree to which we live our daily lives in the absence of the cross is the degree to which we forget. Our sensitivity to life in the Spirit becomes dulled and our conscience clouded, and we carry on in the old ways as if the dead body were alive.

The reality of this struggle faces us every day in the form of a choice. "Therefore do not let sin reign in your mortal body so that you obey its evil desires," warned Paul. "Do not offer the parts of your body to sin, as instruments of wickedness, but rather offer yourselves to God, as those who have been brought from death to life" (Romans 6:12–13).

This opportunity of choice is ever before us. It is what I call the "as if" of the Christian walk. Yes, Christ has died for all our sins past, present, future. Yes, we have risen with him in newness of life. Yes, we still carry around a body of death. Yes, we can choose death or life at any time. Walk then, *as if* the life has happened. Walk *as if* the dead thing is dead, and the Spirit is alive. Live in the "as if," and you will walk in the truth.

But it is impossible to do this without the cross ever before us. The cross in the center of our daily lives will protect us from falling into either one of two common traps. One is the trap of returning to the callousness of a life of sin (impossible to do if the sacrifice of Christ has any foothold in my mind); the other trap is the opposite extreme, thinking that a Christian is somehow beyond sin altogether—that a state of sinless perfection is attainable in this life. People who believe this distort the Word of God and deny the Scriptures that clearly talk of a continual struggle with sin that believers can expect.[3]

Both of these errors lead us to live a lie. Christians who are consciously sinning are lying against their own consciences and grieving the Holy Spirit. They are making a mockery of the cross and trampling on the grace of God. It would be better for these people, and for everyone, for them to leave the fold of Christianity, if even for a season, and sin with great vigor. At least they would have a clearer conscience, and we who are trying to walk in the Spirit would not have the opportunity of their bad example in the camp to justify our own shifty feet.

---

[3]See Romans 7:7–25; Romans 8:22–25; 1 John 1:8–10; 2 Corinthians 4:10–11.

On the other hand, Christians who believe they are beyond sin lie about life as it actually is and perpetuate a false holiness that makes a sham of the gospel. These folks make the grace of God unnecessary, in that their own righteousness is adequate for the job.

In both cases the cross directs us back to the truth. The hymn writer has pictured the believer clinging to the old rugged cross, and it is impossible to cling to such a cross without getting splinters. Thank God for splinters. Those splinters cut into the conscience and keep us honest. They keep us closer to living life realistically. As Oswald Chambers has stated so well: "The test of the life of a saint is not success, but faithfulness in human life as it actually is."[4]

"Life as it actually is" is fraught with choices. It presents me with a death that masquerades as life and a real resurrected life that sometimes seems remote. And it is a life full of distractions that would lead me away from dealing with this issue at all, distractions that would so occupy my time as to postpone this choice altogether. This state is the worst of all. About the only thing that keeps us from being distracted is the cross, planted right in the middle of everything.

That cross constantly reminds me that I died there with Christ, and in order to live in his life, I must see myself nailed up there. My rights, my comfort, and my own needs have spikes driven through them. They belong up there, not here in my grasp where I pamper and play up to them.

The day is coming when the struggle will be over, but there is no hiding place down here for my comfortable self.

---

[4]Oswald Chambers, *My Utmost for His Highest* (New York: Dodd, Mead, & Company, Inc., 1935), 321.

I don't coddle myself; I skewer myself to a cross. "Those who belong to Christ Jesus have crucified the sinful nature with its passions and desires" (Galatians 5:24). Paul clearly indicates that I do this to myself. In order to love my wife as Christ loved the church and gave himself up for it, I must climb up on a cross and give myself up there just as Christ did. This wasn't easy for him. He sweat drops of blood as he faced the reality of the Crucifixion.

Can I expect it to be any easier for me? I think I have. I think we as Christians have all been too easy on ourselves.

This is nothing short of in-the-trenches, courageous work. Saying no to yourself is the hardest thing you will ever do. You have to be ruthless. When the Spirit of God gives you the slightest indication that some thought or action or attitude might be wrong, that's when you nail it. Don't give it a chance to live. It will be just as bloody as the death of Christ. Not a pretty sight.

God, like a western bounty hunter, is going to bring every one of his subjects in, dead or alive. Dead because we never died to self. Alive because we learned to do the dirty work of dying daily to our rights and privileges so that his life could be manifested in us.

In order for me to live unto God, I must daily put to death this body of sin. I must learn to give up the grip I have on my ego—or God, out of his great love for me, will take it from me through a process of pain and humiliation. He will leave me no choice but to let go of it.

If the ultimate fate of this body of sin is its crucifixion, then we might as well stop fighting and get on with it. Only then can we start to experience a daily life of faith.

I had a hard time taking this truck back. Returning it meant I was going to have to come down to driving close to the road again, back to unpacking all those boxes and figuring out where their contents go, back to the desk in the same shape I left it in before I moved, back to reminders of disappointment, questions I have no answers for, and destinations far more complex than a stop on the highway or the end of the street. I have country to travel here where there are no roads and, consequently, no maps.

This, then, is the real test. It's not found in the spotlight or the limelight; it's found in the study light under which I have arranged my desk and the things that occupy it. The real test is not found in the rush of battle out there on the big front as much as it is here, fighting to get beyond myself so I can care about the lives of those within reach of me. It's not how I fare with audiences of various sizes and backgrounds that counts but how I fare with my wife and children and close friends, here where faces have names and words carry real expectations.

It takes little giving up to be what I am on the road— hardly any dying to self. There I am the star. I am someone. In fact, I am the expected one. They've been waiting for me to arrive. Everything revolves around me and my message. Here at home, few care about me and my message the way they do elsewhere, and that's the way it should be. There is no one to coddle me. Here I am surrounded by other lives than mine, with other messages no less important. If I am going to live and love here, I am going to have to give myself up. I am going to have to die—to pick up my cross and follow Christ's example. I am going to have to get by the barriers of my selfishness and egocentrism and step over the dead body to get to those around me that I truly love. This is not impossible. I can do this because Christ has already done it, and he is waiting to have my permission to do it again through me. He is waiting to bring himself alive in me.

Now when a truck passes and I look over next to me, I don't even sense it's a truck. I don't see the man in the cab; I don't feel the power of its massive rolling load. I can't even read the name on the side of the door. I only see the top of a very big wheel, and I plan to give it plenty of room.

10

DEATH OF THE UNKNOWN SELF

THE DEATH OF SELF is the crux of the daily life of a saint, yet as both a concept and a spiritual discipline it has always been difficult to understand, much less accept. It's no wonder. Dying to self has a battle on at least three fronts.

Human nature stands against it because any death is painful and humiliating. As someone once said, "Everyone wants to get to heaven but nobody wants to die."

Second, our culture, even a dangerously large proportion of current Christianity, opposes the death of self in favor of a host of self-embracing philosophies that qualified the '80s as the "me" generation and the '90s as the "age of self."

And Satan and his forces oppose it—all the enemies of God who know that the death of self leads to the one thing they abhor the most: a life in the Spirit, a life of joy and love and kindness, giving and sacrifice, self-control, and abandonment to God. Awful words in the ears of demons, to be sure. Don't underestimate the power of the underworld in attempting to confuse believers on this issue.

Because of this, you and I as average Christians have to work our way through a labyrinth of subtle diversions that would lead us away from the simple reality of the death of self. One such diversion was brought to light for me recently by a brief exposure to the theories of the famous psychologist Dr. Carl Jung.

Carl Gustav Jung (1875–1961) was a Swiss psychiatrist and psychologist who believed that human behavior is largely influenced in unknown ways by the unconscious part of the mind. His theories of the workings of the mind, though not Christian in intent, helped me to discover a major misconception in my evangelically trained thinking.

Hardly anyone would argue against the proposition that our minds are made up of degrees of conscious and unconscious thought. It is a substantiated fact that we use a very small percentage of our mental capacities at any given time. If selfhood were a full bottle of wine, what we usually spend our time thinking and talking about would occupy only the neck of the bottle. The rest would remain untouched and largely a mystery.

Jung equates the ego with the conscious part of self, usually choking back the larger, unconscious part just as the neck of the bottle holds back the wine. What he calls the "larger self" is what we might call our "real self"—that part of us that may or may not be in keeping with the image of ourselves we are consciously trying to put forth. As Jung explains it, the larger self is where the connections to God and others are made. Christians would probably interpret this larger self as the place where the Spirit dwells in us.

For this larger or "real" self to be known, according to

Jung, the ego must be freed of its egocentricity; the protective small neck of the bottle must be forced open (i.e., broken) to let the rest of the wine out. This process of gradually bringing the subconscious to the conscious level—of bringing one's self to the forefront—is called self-actualization, the process by which, according to Dr. Jung, a person becomes whole. But this self-disclosure is made more difficult by the fact that the larger self (the deeper part of the bottle) is also where the darker self (what Christians would simplistically call the sin nature) resides. Thus wholeness, even in Jung's secular view, is obtained along a somewhat rugged path. It necessitates a breaking of the ego, or conscious self, and a confrontation with one's feared darker side.

Reading Jung's theory is almost like reading a book on the cross that has everything but the cross in it. We need only to fill in the blanks. At one point, for instance, he talks about the need for the protective small neck of ego to be forced open by catastrophic acts of God or by a soul voluntarily putting itself into a situation where it knows it will lose its egocentrism. The desired results, though painful, are a conscious or unconscious choice.

In more ways than one, Jung's theories can be looked upon as a psychological description of the struggle of a soul facing the cross. His illustration of a personality becoming whole is surprisingly close to what happens when someone encounters and submits to the cross and its work on a daily basis. Self is broken; sin is faced; connections are made with God and with others who are walking the same road; and however painful this might be, it is all part of the process of becoming whole and of releasing the life of the Spirit in us.

Jung's model also affords an almost comical look at what happens when someone resists this same work of the cross in their lives. His picture of the conscious mind maintaining a tight hold on the subconscious for fear of what might be known or uncovered there is an all-too-familiar image of the mind of the average Christian. How often I have found myself holding back what I fear might be known or discovered in the dark recesses of my soul, clinging tightly to a certain Christian ideal of myself that I am consciously trying to present. As Christians, we are always maintaining a tight hold on the conscious part of our minds. The neck of the bottle is where we have learned to think pure thoughts, fight off those that aren't so pure, analyze our actions, accuse and defend ourselves, and compare ourselves to other Christians to maintain a relative measurement of how we are doing.

The subconscious, on the other hand, is something the typical Christian does not trust at all. In fact, we have come to believe that the subconscious is the seat of all the evil in our lives. All the bad things (evil thoughts, lustful desires, selfish ambitions) come from some unknown place inside of us that we are supposed to keep under control. Awful things rise up out of the evil dungeon of the subconscious whenever we start to get lazy and let our minds slip into places where we should not let them go. We are supposed to be occupying our conscious thoughts with good things—which would be fine, if it were only possible to do.

Instead, a picture of the constricted Christian (like the "church lady" of *Saturday Night Live*) begins to come into focus. This is the classic portrayal of a closed-minded, small-necked, pursed-lips sort of person battling decadence, sin, and immorality on every side while most likely losing the most important battle in her own mind. This person is doing everything possible to concentrate on all things good and pure and right, while at the same time trying to hold down an evil nature that rears its ugly head from within. And the unfortunate creatures who have to come in contact with such a person end up being the sad benefactors of this moral inconsistency.

The remarkable thing is that such a person—we'll call her the "church lady" for the sake of an admitted stereotype—can actually get away with thinking she has died to self. This is hard to imagine until you encounter Jung's theories. The church lady believes her problem is her sin nature, and she agrees that it needs to die. However, as far as she is concerned, that nature dwells in the subconscious part of her mind. It's a part of the larger self she is holding back with her protective, thin-necked ego. She reads all the Scriptures about dying with Christ, and she interprets them as referring to the dark part of her that has died.

This is a neat little trick. Christians who think their struggle with an evil nature is largely in the region of the subconscious will have a relatively easy job disposing of it. If the seat of all of the church lady's evil is in the subconscious, then let it die. She can beat on it as much as she wants; it's no skin off her back. This kind of death is no more life-threatening than beating on a pillow. She doesn't even have to know what's dying, since what she is putting to death is in the subconscious part of her mind anyway. Kill it a hundred times over, it doesn't matter.

I remember thinking like this and actually believing I was dying to self. As long as this death can be put in terms of a *part of me* (the "old man," the "old self," or the "sin nature") and not *me*, I can "die" and never have this death affect me. I can whale away religiously on that wicked, nebulous, sinful nature and never feel the force of the blow.

We can easily see how this becomes a useless exercise that has no basis in reality. There is no humility produced by this activity, no brokenness, and no real facing of sin—but most importantly, *no death*. The subconscious self is merely a straw man I get to execute while my conscious ego goes untouched. In other words, I can "die to sin" without ever having to know or face anything sinful in my life. I can "die to sin" without ever having to be humbled by the cross. This death of the unknown self is nothing more than a mental exercise—spiritual gymnastics in the realm of the subconscious. And like those carnival games where you try to smash rabbits popping up and down out of holes, the real sin in my life keeps slipping back under before I can ever deal it a good blow.

The church lady may believe she has died to her self by thinking of the "old man" as dead, but her self-righteous ego hasn't died at all. It isn't even ill. It's in full operation, in fact: comparing, judging, and engaged in the task of protecting itself. This kind of Christianity has not made anything better. It has only made things worse, because this person is in denial without really knowing it while at the same time dangerously in possession of all the right answers. This thinking ultimately makes people islands, cut off from God, from others, and from their own inner sin nature in an attempt to keep themselves pure.

Any talk of crucifying the "old man," the "old self," or the "sin nature" must be suspect. Even though these terms are used in the Scriptures, they have generally become to us nothing more than euphemisms for subconscious sin—sin we do not want to have to face or deal with by name. Facing real sin by name could be humiliating. It could be damaging to our ego. It might mean that we would have to actually die. Welcome to the truth.

"I have been crucified with Christ," Paul said in Galatians 2:20, "and I no longer live, but Christ lives in me." What does he mean here? Part of me was crucified and part of me lives? Which part is which? Can I divide myself up like this?

It's actually not as complicated as it sounds. *All* of me dies so that *all* of me can live on an entirely different basis. I lived for me until I died, Paul is saying, and now that I am dead, I have no other reason to live, indeed, no other way of living—no other one to live for, but to live for Christ and by faith in Christ. And if I should forget about this and go back to living for myself again as if I were alive to me, there is a cross around to remind me that this body I carry is dead. And if there isn't a cross around, I might want to put one up in a prominent location as a reminder.

Dying to self is a real death that takes place in my conscience, in my plans, in the way I order my day, and especially in the relationships that are closest to me. It is a death to my ego. It is the end of centering my world, my time, and my relationships around me. It has to be my real conscious self that dies, or I will never be able to step over this dead body and get on with my life in the Spirit.

Dying to self is admitting that I am the problem. I need

to be delivered from me. My conscious self is constantly focusing on one increasingly boring subject—me—and I desire and seek deliverance from this selfish ego. There is only one way for this to happen. I must die. Not some mysterious unknown me that lurks in the recesses of my soul, but the all-too-well-known me. The one I go around and around with in my conscious mind. My conscious self must die in order to reveal the sin in me that must be dealt with. What has to die is the very hold I have on myself. It is spiritual idealism cracking open, loosening its hold, watching the ideal shatter as the real truth about me pours out.

As Jung pointed out, this humbling encounter usually happens when I face some catastrophic act of God. But I would hate to think that my wholeness was waiting on a national disaster to express itself. The cross, if we truly face it, is disaster enough. It's a universal disaster for Christ and a personal disaster for us where we are forced to face the real catastrophe of our sin. The cross, properly visited, brings our sin to the surface. We become conscious of it. The thing we feared is known, yet only then can we be made whole. Only in facing our sin can we ever be forgiven.

Jung also believed that this process of bringing one's self out to the forefront necessitated a confrontation with one's feared darker side. But without Christ and a cross and the forgiveness offered there, who could live through this death?

We cannot live through this encounter without someone there with us. This is the glory of the cross. Christ has gone through this before us. He knows what death is like. He's seen the awful face. He's seen the worst of it—worse than you or I will ever have to see. And he got through to the other side.

For this reason, I find hope in the cross. There is no horror so great that the cross has not seen it, no pride so mighty that the cross cannot bring it down. The cross humbles and the Spirit exalts all those who are brought low by it. When Jesus said that the proud will be humbled and the humble will be exalted, he was not only speaking of types of people. He was speaking of a process that would accompany all who meet him at the cross.

We can all come to the cross and be found out. There is nothing to fear, for death has been conquered and sin has been paid for. The only thing to be feared at the cross is loss of pride and position, and anyone who can't afford to lose these would not be happy at the cross anyway. The present reality of the cross both breaks us and allows us to be broken.

But in that brokenness, we discover more than what we could ever bargain for. We come expecting judgment and receive mercy; we come expecting death and receive life; we come expecting rejection and find acceptance; we come knowing we are dirty and receive cleansing for our sins.

When the soldier pierced Jesus on the cross, he was surprised to find both blood and water flowing out of his wounded side. Both are necessary for us—the blood of death and the water of life. The blood is a sacrifice for sin; the water is a cleansing from sin. And when we come to the cross, both blood and water reach us at the same time.

We can attend church, sing hymns to God, worship, and contemplate spiritual things from the neck of the bottle up. But when we face ourselves as we truly are, when we are broken and poured out before him, we become open as well to a larger understanding and experience of God. When we face the cross and see our real sins—the conscious, known sins, the ones we can put real names to—then we can receive from him a real forgiveness and a deeper love than we ever thought possible. This love rushes to fill the deepest cut sin and guilt has made in our lives. This love shows us that God was thinking about us long before we ever thought about him. This love is big enough and powerful enough to swallow up all our sin because it has already done just that on the cross. This love grows out of knowing we are loved in spite of ourselves. This love washes us clean.

Such love could only have a name called "grace."

11

THE GRACE LINE

"HI, JOHN, this is Grace. Just wanted to let you know I was down here." It was 5:27 A.M., and she was right on time. A few minutes early, in fact. It was a good thing, too, because I had failed to get her phone number the night before, and I would have had no way to get to the airport if she hadn't shown up.

There is no way she could have known how significant a statement her words were for me at the time. She was merely following through with her assignment to pick me up at my hotel room and drive me to the airport for an early morning flight home. She was a member of the church group I had sung for the previous night and had volunteered for taxi service. I hadn't even remembered her name until she said over the phone, "Hi, John, this is Grace. Just wanted to let you know I was down here."

Those simple words hit me in an entirely different manner than she could have intended. For her it was a casual statement, probably her first words of the morning except for ordering coffee with two creams and a sugar at the twenty-four-hour market on the way to my hotel. But for me, those words were the words of God, breathed to me over the in-house telephone line of my hotel by the Holy Spirit, catching me totally by surprise in their directness and disarmament of worry and guilt: "Hi, John, this is Grace. Just wanted to let you know I was down here."

I had only been awake for half an hour, yet I had somehow managed in that short space of time to put myself into a guilt trip that was taking me further and further away from the truth. I woke up with baggy eyes, regretting a choice I had made the night before, and I was already working myself over for it. It seemed like a harmless thing at first—staying up late in my room to watch TV—but that was after telling the sponsor I wasn't available to go out after the concert with some of the members of the group because I had such an early flight the next morning.

What if God had wanted me to be with those people, and I, in effect, had lied to them because I came back to my room and stayed up for two hours anyway? Not to mention that my TV viewing had no redeeming qualities, and not to mention that the schedule I was under allowed for only a minimum of sleep for the next few weeks. Not to mention the demands of being separated from my family and knowing I did not have a moment to waste on myself.

And now I was starting a new day off on the wrong foot already, bemoaning my lack of sleep and having all these guilty thoughts clogging up the beginning of another day—as if ruining the night before wasn't enough.

That's when the phone rang, and a voice out of nowhere

said, "Hi, John, this is Grace. Just wanted to let you know I was down here."

There is nothing to compare with the concept of grace as it comes to us from God. Even the sound of the word itself suggests its beauty. When I hear the word *grace* I think of ballet dancers, a Mozart symphony, a pure white swan gliding on a glassy lake, or the sound of French being spoken softly in the corner of a quiet restaurant. Even in a theology book, *grace* carries itself with great beauty. It is a golden thread woven through history by which God carries out his plan of redemption.

Like a phone call from God, grace always has a way of stopping us dead in our tracks. We will always be surprised by it, because there is nothing natural about grace—nothing we can plan on or take for granted. Grace always catches us by surprise because we keep reverting to our old ways of achieving approval and acceptance.

We have no human counterpart for grace. Grace is something that God has given totally of his own free will. It is God's decision to be favorable to us; it has everything to do with his choice and nothing to do with our favorable rating. We are so programmed to interact on a performance basis with others—even with ourselves—that we have no mechanism in our makeup with which to interpret the real meaning of grace. We can try to put it into words and definitions, but we will never fully grasp it. It has its origin totally in the character of God. We have nothing to do with it.

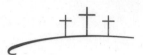

Years ago I took out a personal loan with a businessman who was an elder of my church. As the years passed and finances tightened, I made on-again, off-again payments on the debt. My record was not good. Not too long ago, with about half of this loan paid off when it should have been ancient history, he came up to me at a wedding, put his arm around me, and announced that he was canceling my debt.

Nothing like this had ever happened to me before. There is no way to explain it apart from the overflowing generosity of this man's heart. There was no reason to ask or even think of the debt being cancelled—nothing in me that deserved it. Based on my performance on the loan, I deserved a call from a collection agency instead.

Even more remarkable was the way in which he did it. There was not the slightest indication of reluctance on his part—no final dig at my poor performance, no token speech for me to get my act together, no last lesson. The tone of his voice told me that this act was something he had come to on his own. It had nothing to do with me. There was nothing but pleasure in his announcement of this to me, and for me to have hesitated in accepting it would have been to deny his joy. I could no more deny him than the prodigal son could deny his father's welcome at his return. The son tried to apologize, to explain why he came home to try and make amends, but his father would have none of it. The son's little speech was virtually smothered in his father's joy.

Whenever I need a reminder of what God's grace is like, I pull out the original promissory note we both signed when I borrowed this money. Written, circled, and dated across the face of it are these words: "Paid in full."

Wait a minute, I always remember. *I did not pay this bill in full. I performed poorly on this bill.* Yet there it is, before my very eyes, signed and dated by the lender: "Paid in full." And if I did not pay this debt, then he did. He paid it because he wanted to.

Grace is just like this. "Paid in full" was written and circled in blood across the debt of my sin. The payment required was death, but God paid it instead. And he paid it for no other reason than the fact that he wanted to.

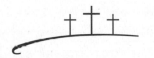

I knew immediately that the voice speaking to me over the phone was a setup by God. He was playing a joke on me—probably chuckling to himself while he arranged this. *Grace is downstairs waiting.*

How often we refuse to believe this and stay upstairs with our worry and our guilt. Grace is downstairs waiting to pick us up and move us on, but we want to punish ourselves, to pay the price of our own sin. We want to feel bad for a few days so we can feel better about blowing it. And as if this weren't enough, we like sitting on other people's badness so we can feel better about our own.

Without knowing it, we can become like the teachers of the law and the Pharisees. "You shut the kingdom of heaven in men's faces," Jesus said. "You yourselves do not enter, nor will you let those enter who are trying to" (Matthew 23:13). If we're not going to be accepting God's grace for ourselves, chances are we aren't going to let anyone else get any, either.

The church lady certainly isn't getting any, that's for sure. Her phone has been ringing; she just hasn't picked it up for a long time. Even if she did, she might not recognize the voice or the message. Her problem is that she's dealing with this in a whole different manner than grace. "With the measure you use, it will be measured to you" (Matthew 7:2). And with the way she has been measuring out judgment, the church lady has already decided what judgment she wants to receive.

Elsewhere, Christ said: "Blessed are the merciful, for they will be shown mercy" (Matthew 5:7). He's saying, "You call the shots. You decide how you want me to deal with you. If you want me to measure out a judgment on each thought and action, then measure each other that way. If you want me to be merciful to you, then be merciful to each other."

Grace can be very dangerous. It means that righteousness is out of our control. It means we can't have it both ways. We can't put everyone else under the law while we stay under grace. No, grace is very messy. You get it before you've fixed yourself up, before you've learned your lesson, before you've paid the price, and you have to give it out the same way: "Forgive us our debts as we forgive our debtors."

The truth of the matter is, we're all in this together.

We've all failed; we've all fallen short. "Oh God, we have sinned," Billy Graham said. And yet for all of us, there is a provision called grace, and in this desperation, in the total need for this grace, we are all the same. We all line up at the heavenly soup kitchen for this meal.

This is why grace is such a dangerous thing. You never know who might qualify for it. I'm sure we are all in for a big surprise when we get to heaven and find out who is there—all those people who were invited in off the streets because the ones who received invitations to the banquet were too busy with their own righteous things that they had to do. And who are all these scoundrels at the table? They're the ones who heard the phone ring and picked it up.

There's a hot line in the White House, a cellular line in the car, a toll-free line for business. How about a "grace line" for all of us? Need a call on the grace line? Go ahead; it's ringing. It always is. Whatever you're up to, I think you need this call today. I think we all need this call as many times as we can remember to pick up the phone.

Go ahead; pick it up. I know what you're going to hear: "Hi, this is Grace. Just wanted to let you know I was down here."

Recently I found—amid the legal requirements of the Ten Commandments of all places—an old covenant statement of God's grace. It says that God visits his wrath to the fourth generation, but visits his mercy on a thousand generations. That is Scripture's way of saying that God is more liberal with his mercy than he is severe in his judgments. The Scriptures do speak of the wrath of God, the Ten Commandments still stand, and you and I still break them and experience real guilt and fear God's judgment. But the wrath of God always has compassion and mercy bleeding through it somewhere. We are surprised by his grace all over again. This is the present-tense experience of the cross.

There is no escaping this process. To pull grace away from its relationship to sin and judgment is to pull the golden thread out of the fabric and expect it to mean something by itself. Grace means nothing without the law. Grace has to stay near the cross where a real price had to be paid and a real judgment made.

Without the promissory note over which he could have taken me to court, the businessman's payment of my debt would have been unnecessary. I could simply have walked away. The law holds us; grace sets us free.

12

THE CONFESSIONS OF ASAPH

*When my heart was grieved and my spirit embittered, I
was senseless and ignorant; I was a brute beast before you.*

Psalm 73:21–22

WHEN WE GET BEFORE GOD, draw near the cross, and
see ourselves as we really are, we had best tell the truth
about what we see. This is called confession. It has very little to do with saying we are sorry and a whole lot to do
with telling it like it is.

In this particular psalm, Asaph, the writer and musician, certainly didn't mince any words about his attitude
before God. He began this psalm with: "Surely God is good
to Israel, to those who are pure in heart. But as for me, my
feet had almost slipped" (vv. 1–2). Rarely do we find this
degree of honesty among Christians today.

Asaph, at the time of this writing, was feeling neither
pure in heart nor blessed of God. It is encouraging to find
someone in the Bible juxtaposing himself against such obvious spiritual expectancies. This is a musician, a prophet,
and a poet, and he is not going to give us any baloney
about his being spiritual when he is not.

"For I envied the arrogant when I saw the prosperity of the wicked. They have no struggles" (vv. 3–4). The assumption that the wicked have no struggles is probably not true, but this was the way Asaph saw it, and it's certainly how I see it sometimes. The wicked have it all, and they have it easy. It always gets my goat when someone else is doing well and I'm not. And what makes it worse is when the guy who's doing well is not half as spiritual as I am.

"This is what the wicked are like—always carefree, they increase in wealth. Surely in vain have I kept my heart pure; in vain have I washed my hands in innocence" (vv. 12–13). Now he's really into it deep. He's being self-righteous to the point of self-pity. Self-righteousness doesn't get more ugly than this. "Look at all I've given up for God, and yet these arrogant bleeps get all the wealth and success. And what do I get? Nothing!"

This is the true report of a man confessing his sins. He didn't hold anything back. He was being completely honest about his attitudes before God. We would all be a lot better off if we were as honest as this man. This is someone God could work with because he was telling the truth. Confession brings us in line with the truth. Asaph was not wasting anyone's time saying what he was supposed to say. He was saying what he felt, even though it revealed an inner bitterness and self-pity—attitudes we can all identify with.

"When my heart was grieved and my spirit embittered, I was senseless and ignorant; I was a brute beast before you" (vv. 21–22). Doesn't this sound a little like Paul caught in the classic struggle: "When I want to do good, evil is right there with me" (Romans 7:21)? If Asaph and Paul, separated by a few thousand years and a cross, have similar stories, I can expect to know this struggle myself. It is an age-old struggle, a familiar part of a believer's daily walk of choices.

My son, even at the age of two, was aware of this struggle. Once he was caught lying, thrust face-to-face with the scrutinizing look of his mother. He thought quickly and then came up with: "Well, you see, Mama, there are these two good bugs and three bad bugs in my head," he said, pointing to his outnumbered but clever conscience. "And the two good bugs . . . went out to lunch!" Sometimes I feel as if he even got the odds right, were it not for the Spirit.

The beginning of Asaph's comfort starts here: that his heart was grieved. *What was right* about Asaph was disturbed about *what was wrong*. Or as Paul put it, "For in my inner being I delight in God's law; but I see another law at work in the members of my body, waging war against the law of my mind" (Romans 7:22–23). The desire for the right was present in him, proof of the fact that God had already done a good work in his heart. Asaph's heart was grieved about his bitter spirit. That much he could say for himself. We truly should start worrying when we are no longer grieved by the wrong things we do or say or think.

Once you have tasted of righteousness, once you have the Spirit in your life, you can't enjoy sin anymore. The thrill is gone. The true dilemma of the Christian is this: Sinning makes you miserable and perfection eludes you. To be a true Christian is to walk in this tension. Christians who want to resolve this by pretending they are always on top of this struggle are simply not telling the whole truth. I no longer believe the picture of happy-go-lucky Christians, smiling their ever-loving way to heaven. I'm not sure I ever did.

Asaph's picture is truthful. He even calls himself "a brute beast." When I first read this my mouth dropped open. I had to check and make sure I was reading the Bible. Now *this* is confession. Not only was he honest with God, he was honest with himself. The neck of the bottle broke, and all the ugly stuff poured out. Yet the confession was healing, because he remembered in the process of revealing himself who God was. Along the way, he remembered. He even went into the sanctuary to remember (v. 17).

He went into the sanctuary.... Was that by any chance a church in Old Greenwich, Connecticut, that has a cross right in the middle of it? I know that sanctuary. I walked into that church like a brute beast before God, and I was convinced of it right away.

This psalm, of course, was written before the cross, which makes its conclusion even more remarkable ... and yet not so remarkable. The cross is for all time and reaches in all directions.

"I was a brute beast before you. Yet I am always with you; you hold me by my right hand. You guide me with your counsel, and afterward you will take me into glory" (vv. 22–24). There it is: an old covenant statement of grace if I ever heard one. God is going to take a brute beast with him right into heaven. That is impossible without the cross. And yet Asaph, on the other side of the cross from us, was counting on it. He was counting on the fact that God would figure out some way to accept him as he was, for he could do no other. This is a pre-cross expectation of grace, and Asaph didn't even know what to call it.

Grace, Asaph. It's a beautiful word, isn't it? And you got it anyway, buddy.

Asaph began this psalm with: "But as for me, my feet had almost slipped." He ends it, "But as for me, it is good to be near God" (v. 28). What a difference! This is a God who holds my right hand when I am a beast, who takes walks with me and listens to my embittered soul. This is a God whose judgment is tempered by his mercy. This is a God who gives my failing heart strength, and regardless of what is happening in this unstable world: "It is good to be near him."

And I say from this side of the cross, after reading what Asaph wrote, that it is good to be near the cross. It is good to be able to have access to this kind of honesty with God. It is good to talk through my feelings and emotions even when they are not what they are supposed to be, because in the process, I will finally see myself as I really am and agree with God about what I see. And then I will remember that in spite of being who I am, he is always with me. I will remember that I have no one else in heaven but him and I desire nothing on earth but to know him.

13

THE DEATH OF MAUVE

I JUST CAUGHT AN article in the *Los Angeles Times* about the latest resurgence of color schemes in the ever-circling history of design. Remember those avocado greens and mustard yellows from the '60s we've all been dying to see again? It would appear that mauve is already on the way out. If this is true, some churches are going to have a bit of remodeling to do. Some of them probably still have their carpets on order. Maybe it's not too late to change the color.

As the church faces the beginning of the twenty-first century, we find it almost suffocating with relevancy and not yet able to admit its longing for what is real and lasting amid a constantly shifting culture. Has relevancy, like the color mauve, run its course?

At the end of the '60s era, Don McLean wrote and recorded a sweeping critique of the history of pop music in one song called "American Pie," in which he lamented the "day the music died." No one is sure exactly what day that was, but at some level Don McLean was right. Something did die. And now, as we hear oldies stations across the radio dial playing music from this era all polished up and re-released on compact disc (even McLean's song, which I heard yesterday in a supermarket), it sounds to me as if the music is twice dead.

The spontaneity and the protest are gone. The reaching and stretching into something new is gone. The grunginess of the sound is gone. The youth and life that breathed out through this music is gone. It was lost somewhere in the remix. Even much of new music being made today seems to be made up of body parts and limbs of all this other music that died, and what was once the breaking of the rules is now the new rule to follow. Now music is made in an expensive studio to sound as if it had been recorded in a garage, where twenty years ago they just recorded it in a garage. Maybe there are no more rules to break, and we have to keep resuscitating what died over and over again.

Christianity in the new millennium needs to take a cue from this cultural saturation. Maybe we need our own "American Pie" song.

I couldn't resist. I messed around with Don McLean's pie recipe and came up with the following:

Bye-bye, Christian culture, bye-bye . . .
Drove my Ford for the Lord
Till the gas tank went dry.
Them industry types are drinkin' Perrier and lime,
Singin': "This could be the day that I die."
Bye-bye, gospel pie in the sky . . .
Drove my Ford for the Lord
But my gas tank went dry.
Now stars in their cars grab a piece of the prize,
And a preacher can cash in on the pie.

Christianity hasn't died, of course, nor has the contemporary expression of faith suffered any noticeable setback. In fact, such expressions appear to be in excellent health at the moment. No, what actually died is the hope that contemporary Christianity might mean anything in the real world as we have come to know it.

There was a time when being contemporary in the realm of faith was the new thing. It was an attention-getter on its own. Popular songs and contemporary stylings of faith used to turn people's heads. Contemporary faith used to be countercultural, as the gospel has always been. Now being contemporary and cultural is the norm of the average church. It is expected. But like "modern" architecture of the '60s that now looks like something out of the original *Star Trek* series, even the word *contemporary* seems dated. Everybody is contemporary now, and when everyone is contemporary, *contemporary* ceases to mean anything in and of itself. You don't get points anymore for being a contemporary church.

Contemporary Christian culture is now just another blip on the map, a niche in someone's marketing plan, a bull's-eye on a targeting campaign, a gold mine for a conservative political agenda, or a mailing list in someone's data bank. Contemporary Christianity, in short, has been swallowed up by the culture it once tried to influence.

A newspaper article in the *Los Angeles Times* quoted Robert Lichter, director of the Center for Media and Public Affairs, as saying that the Clinton Administration "embraced popular culture as part of a general strategy to use it to get their message out." Sound familiar? Then he went on to point out there were pitfalls in such a merger. "The danger is, you can be used up by popular culture, since the entertainment world does not operate by the same rules as the world of politics and journalism." (And well might we add: the kingdom of God.)

This is what I mean by the death of contemporary Christianity. Popular culture has used up whatever contemporary Christianity hoped to gain by this alliance. Christianity has taken up such an identification with culture that it has rolled over and died in respect to the radical, confronting nature of faith and the cross. Like a cross that once held a bleeding Savior and now is an ornament for a pop star or a wall hanging in a mauve church, the message of sin and real guilt and the cross and resurrection of Jesus Christ has blended into the cultural landscape so completely that it no longer clashes with anything. Sin is dysfunctional behavior; guilt is a bad feeling; the cross is God's love song to the world; and the Resurrection is just one more new beginning.

But now that mauve is already on the way out, instead of opting for the next color scheme, this might be an opportune time to put a cross in the middle of whatever we have left and let it be the new statement. With the death of mauve, the vast number of errors in judgment that have occurred as a result of a church trying to be relevant to a contemporary culture could give way to a more poignant and straightforward cross-cultural gospel. Then perhaps the cross could once again stand on its own in the center of everything as the enigma that it truly is.

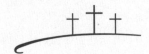

We would all lead more honest lives, corporately and individually, with a cross at the center of everything. The closer we get to the cross, the more transparent we become. Pastors would be more honest if they had to speak through a cross. People would give the gospel a second thought if they had to listen through one. And perhaps with a more visible cross around, sin could be talked about as the common struggle that it is.

Roman Catholics have something on evangelicals on this one. They still have confession. In the old days, confession was secret and faceless, held in the privacy of a dark confessional. Now confessions are more often heard in the priest's office, but they are still private and individual, not part of the larger body. Similarly, some mainline Protestant churches include a general confession in their liturgy.

It's a start. But the Scripture calls for something beyond either of these. "Therefore confess your sins to each other and pray for each other so that you may be healed" (James 5:16). If we are to confess to one another, provision must be made in the church for small enough gatherings of believers where this level of interaction can take place.

Whenever anyone brings up the subject of open confession, however, someone will always say that it's not good for people to air their "dirty laundry" in public. I have never been able to understand this. There is no such thing as a clean sin; we need to confess.

A heavy burden rests on leadership to model an honest struggle with sin. Not through the tear-stained confessions of a leader who got caught, but through the voluntary down-to-earth relating of one who, like everyone else, has to pick his or her way through the mine fields of temptation, a relating that will encourage others to realize that they are not alone in their struggle.

Those who want to honor the gospel have to be ruthless with themselves. The cross cuts deeply into our lives, but it can be known only as far as the knowledge of our sin goes. If we don't make our sin known to ourselves and others, our experience of the cross will be a shallow, sentimentalized version of the real thing.

The cross needs to be brought back to the center of our worship. Worship has been the theme of the church for over a decade, and many of the churches I speak and perform in have a full-time worship leader on staff.

But worship is not an end in itself. Sin cannot be drowned in forty-five minutes of singing. If there is blood on my hands, no amount of worship can wash it off. There is an assumption that worship, if it is "done right," will do something to me. It will take me somewhere I haven't been before—upward, nearer to the presence of God. This is a very attractive concept for people, but it is also dangerous to lead someone to a supposedly spiritual place without having them reckon with their own sin.

True worship takes us low before it ever takes us high. Worship starts at the cross every time. It begins with what I see of myself there and continues on through to my grace and forgiveness. I worship as a forgiven sinner before I worship as a saint. And when I do worship as a saint, it's as an astonished one, knowing the truth about myself.

As a continual reminder of the centrality of the cross, the Lord's Supper needs to be reintroduced to our congregations. The early church broke bread every time they gathered. Jesus said we were to do this as often as we eat of the bread and drink from the cup—that was at least one major meal a day. Once every couple of months is not enough. Returning to the cross roots our worship in history and in what Jesus has done for us, reminding us of just how much we need this forgiveness and new life.

The most meaningful experiences I have had in Communion have always been in a small circle of friends. The most unforgettable of all was a group of singers with whom I had gathered for a seminar. Half a dozen of us found ourselves singing old hymns together into the early morning. When someone suggested we share in Communion, we took whatever was available, blessed it, and passed it around as the Lord's Supper. It was the holiest punch and cookies I'll ever have.

Coming together at the cross also roots our worship in fellowship. True fellowship grows out of facing and confessing our real sins to one another and receiving our forgiveness together. Evangelicals love to perform this process of cleansing separately, away from everyone, so we can then come back together as neat, clean Christian people. But this is not God's way.

"If we walk in the light, as he is in the light, we have fellowship with one another, and the blood of Jesus, his Son, purifies us from all sin" (1 John 1.7). Fellowship grows out of being in the light as Jesus was in it. This is the light that shows us who we really are. It is not always a pleasant thing to stand in this light, yet what a liberating experience to stand there with others and find out we are all the same! We are all sinners, and he died for us all. And, lo and behold, we can take off these dirty garments of death and exchange them for the clean new ones of his righteousness.

This is the process that worship needs to go through every time in order to be real. This is worship with a cross in the middle of it.

Honesty in church is not enough, however. There is an honesty the world needs to see as well. One of the gravest errors Christians can make in an attempt to witness to unbelievers is to try to pass themselves off as some kind of finished product. I can remember as a child always being taught to maintain a good image among non-Christians. I was supposed to be the "after" of the before and after ads for the Sin Watcher's Club of America. We were to show non-Christians our good side for the sake of our testimony to them. Seeing us as such sterling examples of faith was supposed to make them all want to be Christians, too.

Nothing could be further from the truth. This kind of "witness" destroys the gospel and drives people away.

As with believers, our truest witness to the world comes through the cross. There is no double standard. The slightest suggestion that we should act differently in different contexts is an obvious indication that we are not being ourselves in either. The compelling nature of the cross is that "Jesus Christ died to save sinners, of whom I am the chief." That message does not change when we turn and face the world. If anyone needs to see us as forgiven sinners, it is people who don't yet understand the gospel, because in our story, they will find hope for themselves as well. It is not a story of success or achievement. It is not a story of continual victory over every bad thing in our lives. It is not a story of one triumph after another. It is a story of grace, of forgiveness. All of us can find ourselves somewhere in that story, just as all of us can find ourselves at the cross if we are willing to look upon him whom we have pierced.

It is my observation that most non-Christians think they have to be good around Christians. If the only thing Christians have accomplished in the world is to make non-Christians feel uncomfortable, then we have truly failed the gospel by not interpreting the true message of the cross. *"Christians aren't better,"* the revised bumper sticker should read, *"just forgiven."* And the good news of this message is that all who face their sin can be forgiven.

We will always have believers and unbelievers, the church and the world (not necessarily identifiable in the obvious ways). But this imaginary entity of a Christian subculture may not be all we thought it was.

And does it matter, after all? Is it important what happens to contemporary Christianity? Will the truth suffer any because of its loss? Will God be somehow thwarted in his attempts to bring his will on earth as it is in heaven if he doesn't have a contemporary Christian subculture as an aid to help him out? Is the future of the gospel really hanging on a satellite dish or a pop song? Can God still get his work done without any of this stuff? Will the church be able to affect the next generation without mauve carpets?

How about avocado?

14

THE OLD RUGGED CROSS

On a hill far away stood an old rugged cross,
The emblem of suff'ring and shame;
And I love that old cross where the dearest and best
For a world of lost sinners was slain.
In the old rugged cross, stained with blood so divine,
A wondrous beauty I see;
For 'twas on that old cross Jesus suffered and died
To pardon and sanctify me.
So I'll cherish the old rugged cross,
Till my trophies at last I lay down;
I will cling to the old rugged cross,
And exchange it someday for a crown.

George Bennard, 1913

I GREW UP WITH THIS HYMN. It was famous in the old white church with the creaky floors. As a child I always thought this was an old person's hymn. Maybe that was because it had the word "old" in it. Or maybe it was because when we had a Sunday Night Sing, "On a Hill Far Away" always seemed to be the special request of the older people, especially one particular gray-haired gentleman who never requested any other hymn but this one. He always called it "The Old Rugged Cross" even though "On a Hill Far Away" was the title in the hymnal. That always made sense to me. I would have called it "The Old Rugged Cross" too, if it had been up to me. *On a hill far away* appears only once in the song; *the old rugged cross* is mentioned over and over.

My friends and I would roll our eyes at each other when we saw the pastor pick the old man because we knew what was coming. We liked faster, peppier hymns like "He Lives" and "Wonderful Grace of Jesus"—hymns you could bounce along with on the bass answer part in the chorus. But the look on the old man's face when we sang this hymn always spoke of a special love affair with the music and the words.

How can you have a love affair with a cross? How can you cherish an apparatus of execution? How could anyone want to cling to a hard, splintery beam of wood? How is it possible to find beauty in its bloodstained grains? It seems awkward to use such warm, friendly terms when speaking of a death device, but this is merely one more inexplicable aspect of the cross. Sooner or later, if you have found forgiveness there, this cut and planed trunk of a tree actually becomes something cherished.

The old man cherishes this cross because he has found forgiveness there countless times, and he knows he can always come to it again. This does not give him license to sin; it is just downright realistic. He doesn't walk away from the cross planning the details of his next sin; he just knows himself. He knows that any solution to the problems in his life that does not take his future sins into account is going to drive him away from reality.

Knowing we're already forgiven could be an opportunity for sin, yet it seems to be a chance the Lord has taken with us. For the old man, the knowledge that he can sin and it will be forgiven makes him not want to sin. His forgiveness is a valuable possession that he has been entrusted with. He does not want to abuse it. As Paul would say it, his freedom makes him want to be a slave. Freedom from sin; slave to Christ.

When I pull out my unpaid bill just to make sure it still has "Paid in Full" written across it, that does not make me want to go out and borrow more money and be irresponsible with it so I can tax someone else's patience and see what I can get away with. Rather, it makes me want to live in a way that would show I was worthy of this trust. It makes me want to avoid putting myself in this position again.

The old man cherishes the cross because he has faced his worst there and has not been turned away. There is no love greater than this: to be loved before you've done anything to earn it. To be smothered in love even before you got to give your acceptance speech. To know that the love was there first, even before you got home—to realize, in fact, that your father was watching for you to come, peering down the driveway, inquiring of passersby if they have seen anything of you. There is nothing you can do to earn this love, nothing you can do to drive it away. And when you finally showed up, rascal that you are, lo and behold, he threw you a party!

The old man knows that the cross has been the deathwood of this love he experiences. He knows his sin cost the Lord greatly, and though he will never comprehend the price, he will gladly receive it. He is not so proud as to turn it away.

The old man cherishes the cross because he received his Savior there and has been received himself. The cross is where it happened, and the cross is why it happened. God would never be able to receive him had there been no sacrifice. But there was. There was a ram caught in the thicket, and the old man was lifted off the dry kindling, set on his feet, and untied to live again. He cherishes this cross because it has given him a chance to live, to laugh, to play hide-and-seek with his father down the mountainside.

And finally, the old man cherishes the cross because each day he finds out more clearly why he needs it in his life. His growing awareness of God in his life is accompanied by a growing awareness of his need. The more he knows, the more he finds out he doesn't know. He understands that to be full is to be emptied again. This is the cycle of death and life that he experiences over and over.

The old man knows all this because this is familiar ground to him—this rocky terrain around the cross. He has found himself there often, like Nicodemus and John and Mary, stumbling his way among the rocks trying to get closer. He has wept and wondered countless times. He has held the blood in his hands, tasted it, felt it burn all the way down, and he has swallowed the flesh. Each time he remembers the cross, he seems to comprehend it less and love it more.

So when he sings about the old rugged cross, he sings about something familiar, as if he is feeling the grain of the wood where it has been rubbed smooth from so many rememberings. His fingers search for the little raises and valleys of the rugged grain, and his eyes come to rest on the rust-red stains where blood has soaked into the thirsty crevices. And if you could see him sing, you could almost imagine him standing there with his arms wrapped around the cross and his old gray head resting gently against it. He would have loved the church in Old Greenwich, Connecticut, because there he would have been able to do that very thing.

15

STARDUST

"WOODSTOCK," JONI MITCHELL'S haunting anthem to the hopes and dreams of the '60s, examines the destiny of the human race. The lyrics picture humanity as golden—even as stardust—yet trapped in the devil's bargain and in need of getting back to the Garden.

Getting back to the Garden is much more difficult than this song indicates. In fact, it's impossible. Even if we could somehow locate the Garden of Eden, the Scriptures say we would be met at the gate by two angels with flaming swords that flash back and forth barring our entrance. There is no way back in. There is only a way forward, and that path leads through sin and pain and suffering and sacrifice and a cross before it ever gets back to anything that resembles Eden.

Yet in the full scheme of things, it is probably for our best that we cannot return. Getting back to the Garden is not what we really want. Even with the Fall and all the damage done, in some ways we are still better off out here. Satan was right about some things. We did have our eyes opened to see good and evil. We are smarter—less naïve than our ancestral parents. The problem is that we not only see good and evil, we know it; we experience it; we are powerless to stop its influence over us.

Seeing good and evil does not mean that we have the wisdom or the power to choose good every time. We walked out of the Garden into a world that is quite over our heads—over our heads in glory, up to our necks in sin.

Still, we walked out able to see both good and evil. To hear most Christians tell it is to get the impression that the fruit turned everything bad. But the Scriptures tell us they ate of the tree of the knowledge of good *and* evil. Evangelical tradition has a tendency to drop the *good* and turn this tree into the knowledge of *evil* only. We have gotten so wrapped up in talking about the sin and evil that entered the world at this point that we forget to note that there was knowledge of good in this fruit as well.

This knowledge of good is still evidenced in humankind. Look at the arts, at education and science, at relief efforts and ecological and humanitarian concerns of the human beings of the world. Look at movie after movie where love and good win out over hate and evil. Look at the non-Christian family down the street who is more loving than their Christian neighbors. Where does all this come from? It comes from men and women who were made in the image of God, who have had their eyes opened to be able to see both good and evil. As Thomas Wolfe so eloquently put it in his novel *Look Homeward, Angel*, though they are lost, they still "seek the great forgotten language, the lost lane-end into heaven, a stone, a leaf, an unfound door. Where? When?"[1]

---

[1]Thomas Wolfe, *Look Homeward, Angel* (New York: Charles Scribner's, 1947), front page.

What was Joni Mitchell talking about when she referred to humankind as *stardust* and *golden*? Where did that idea come from if not from God, if not from the good that she saw with her own eyes? Solomon did not qualify his statement when he said that human beings have eternity in their hearts, yet they "cannot fathom what God has done from beginning to end" (Ecclesiastes 3:11). Unlimited possibilities, limited scope. That is the frustrating situation of human experience—or, as Solomon put it, "the burden God has laid on men." We can see it, but we can't get to it. We can feel it in our hearts, but we can't explain it in our heads.

We *are* stardust; we *are* golden. Joni Mitchell was right. What is wrong with us has nothing to do with intrinsic value. The fact that we are sinners does not mean that we are nothing. It is actually *because* of our value that it matters that something is wrong. Sin is a tragedy because we are worth something. It ultimately destroys us. It brings down a good thing.

Like a falling star, there is a certain glory to a good thing going down. Some atheists blaze into hell with all the human glory they can muster. Head held high, they will take their shots as they come. This is the way they've played it all along; this is the way they will play it out, and God honors their wish. "I Did It My Way," the theme song of hell, deserves some kind of applause, because there is a value being expressed. As C. S. Lewis has said, each one of us is destined to be an everlasting horror or an eternal glory because of our intrinsic value.[2] These are splendid creatures

---

[2]C. S. Lewis, *The Weight of Glory* (Grand Rapids, Mich.: William B. Eerdmans, 1979), 15.

God has created—whatever he does with them and whatever they decide to do with themselves.

All this means that God is in the redemptive business—the process of saving that which was lost, buying back—with the blood of his Son—a people for his own.

The apostle Paul has stated this purpose clearly in Ephesians: "Although I am less than the least of all God's people, this grace was given me: to preach to the Gentiles the unsearchable riches of Christ, and to make plain to everyone the administration of this mystery, which for ages past was kept hidden in God, who created all things. His intent was that now, through the church, the manifold wisdom of God should be made known to the rulers and authorities in the heavenly realms, according to his eternal purpose which he accomplished in Christ Jesus our Lord" (Ephesians 3:8–11).

This is the big picture that God will one day reveal to the universe, the earthly inhabitants he has gathered together as his own—those he has saved through his plan of redemption through the cross. One day, we will all be surrounding him at the throne like stardust.

We are stardust; he is the star, and the shining we display comes from his glory. This plan of God—this incredible mystery that is being worked out for the culmination of all things at the feet of Christ—is for him, not for us.

God has more in mind here than just you and me. Our true meaning and joy comes not in being the focus of all this attention, but in being caught up in it—in being part of the worship. Our true identity is discovered not when we find ourselves, but when we lose ourselves in him.

What God has ultimately planned for us is bigger and

better than anything we could have reclaimed had we made it back to the Garden. That would only have returned us to a state of innocence and ignorance. He has plans for us beyond innocence, beyond the knowledge of good and evil—plans where we partake continually of his life and share in his glory and serve in his universe. Like stardust scattered among the stars, we will shine as an eternal tribute to how far God's love is willing to go to reclaim its object. And throughout eternity we will still be telling the old, old story of Jesus and his love as displayed by his death on the cross and his resurrection from the grave—a story that not even angels comprehend.

EPILOGUE

I AM NOT NOW NOR WILL I ever be the pastor of the Presbyterian church of Old Greenwich, Connecticut. But if I were, I would start a tradition. I would hold a special service on the Saturday before Easter—that dark Saturday sandwiched between Good Friday and Easter Sunday morning when the whole universe held its breath. During that service, we would reflect on the atonement and the mystery of what God accomplished there. How incredible it was of him to set the whole world up this way. Perhaps some members of the congregation would share about the dark Saturdays of the previous year and how they fared through hard times. Maybe some would feel right at home because they were in a dark tomb right then.

Then we would sing. We would sing hymns as Paul and Silas did, like prisoners in the night. We would sing in spite of the fact that it was a dark Saturday and, historically, Jesus was in the tomb—or worse than that, in hell itself. We would sing because we know the story. That is what gives these celebrations meaning. We know how it turns out.

We'd sing songs like:

At the cross, at the cross where I first saw the light,
And the burden of my heart rolled away,
It was there by faith I received my sight,
And now I am happy all the day![1]

Or:

When I survey the wondrous cross
On which the prince of glory died,
My richest gain I count but loss,
And pour contempt on all my pride.[2]

And, of course, we would sing:

Jesus keep me near the cross—
There a precious fountain,
Free to all, a healing stream,
Flows from Calvary's mountain.[3]

Then at the end of the service, in front of everyone, twelve strong men would approach the Old Greenwich cross, pull it out of its socket, and remove it from the room. And in its place on Sunday morning would be an array of Easter lilies the likes of which no one has ever seen before. Each year there would be more lilies than the last until there was no more room in the church on Easter because of all the flowers. So then we would have to take the service outside and welcome the town.

What then? What would be done with the cross after

[1]Ralph E. Hudson (1843–1901), "At the Cross."
[2]Isaac Watts (1674–1748), "When I Survey the Wondrous Cross."
[3]Fanny J. Crosby (1820–1915), "Near the Cross."

Easter? Would it be brought back and lowered down into its socket for another year, or is it no longer necessary in our lives once it has done its work? Given the ongoing preaching of the gospel message, the fact that so many have not truly heard the message of the cross, and the fact that we all, believers or not, need a constant reminder of our sin and what God has done to take care of it, I would want to see it brought back. I would want it to stay there in light of its absence in so many other places in our Christian culture where it needs to be. I would want it there, because once we have experienced God's forgiveness, the cross becomes, in all its mystery and its difficulty, in all its strangeness and incongruity, something to be cherished.

There is one change I would like to see, though. My eleven-year-old daughter did a book of illustrations on the stations of the cross. The last illustration showed an empty cross on a hillside with the sun coming up. Wound around the cross, to about halfway up, was a delicate green plant with bluebell-like flowers. A morning glory had bloomed around the cross right there at the execution site.

I'd like to put a small plant like that at the base of the cross and let it grow a flowering vine up the beam all year long—a reminder of the fact that incredible Sundays always follow Good Fridays just as life swallows death.

STUDY QUESTIONS

Chapter 1

1. How is the cross in the Old Greenwich church like the cross of Christ in our lives?
2. What does the cross represent to most people today?
3. What were your earliest associations with the cross? How did you feel about it?
4. What's the good news/bad news about the cross?
5. How important are history and tradition to faith?
6. What is the cross "in the way of" in your life?

Chapter 2

1. If someone who had no concept of God visited your church for a while, what kind of God would they meet?
2. Why does sacrifice have to be so bloody?
3. What has changed about sacrifice from the Old Testament to today? What hasn't?
4. If you had to slaughter an animal before the pastor and

the congregation every time you wanted to be forgiven for some sin, would that change your life in any way?

5. What if you had to drive a nail into the hand of Jesus for the same reason?

6. What is your favorite spiritual "color"?

Chapter 3

1. How was Christ's death something he did for God alone?

2. What are some pros and cons in attempting to make the gospel relevant to culture?

3. Is the cross relevant to contemporary culture? Why and why not?

4. How do we attempt to make the gospel attractive to the world?

5. What do you think about the statement, "I asked God, 'How much do you love me?' and he stretched out his arms on the cross and said, 'This much'"?

6. How much do you have to understand about the cross to be saved by it?

7. What does the cross say about our worth?

Chapter 4

1. What's wrong with human nature?

2. What's the difference between "sins" and "sin nature"?

3. Why has sin become unpopular today, even in some churches?

4. What are the theological and cultural implications of the statement, "If I'm okay and you're okay, what's he doing up there?"

5. Why do you go to church? (If you don't, why not?)
6. What keeps us from admitting our sin? What happens when we do?

Chapter 5

1. What does it take to see spiritual truth?
2. Have you ever not been able to see something everyone else could see? How did the people who could see it make you feel?
3. Why is it so easy to forget what it was like not to see after your eyes have been opened? Should we forget?
4. Can we do harm to people by making the gospel seem obvious?
5. Why is it hard to live with ambiguity?
6. How can you be more patient with those who can't see?

Chapter 6

1. What strikes you most about the story of Abraham and Isaac?
2. Unlike what he did for Abraham, God made no substitute for his son. What does that tell you about the nature of God?
3. How are we like Isaac?
4. How are we like Abraham?

Chapter 7

1. What's "good" about sin?
2. Why is the cross sin's "antidote"? How does it work? Does it keep on working?

3. Whom do you identify with in the story of Simon and the woman?
4. Is guilt a good or a bad thing?
5. Why are people uncomfortable with the concept of sin?
6. Why does sin need to be personal?
7. What's the difference between Simon's sin and the woman's?

Chapter 8

1. Compare and contrast the experiences of Pilate, Peter, and the three women on that first Easter morning. Why were their experiences so different?
2. In what ways do you "seek the living among the dead" today?
3. How has the resurrection of Christ changed everything?
4. Have you ever been surprised by God?

Chapter 9

1. Why do evangelicals shun symbolism?
2. What role does the cross play in your life once you are a Christian?
3. What does the cross say about my best efforts?
4. How does the cross "kill me"?
5. Contrast your new life in Christ to the old life in your self.
6. What does it mean to die to self?
7. What happens to the old life once it is dead? Do you still carry it around? Can it still influence you? What can you do about this?

Chapter 10

1. What are the similarities between a Jungian theory of "self-actualization" and the biblical doctrine of dying to self?
2. Think of some ways you keep sin in the abstract.
3. How can our sin be brought into our consciousness?
4. Can you list any of your sins by name? What good does this do? Why not just get delivered from your "sins" in general?
5. Why is there nothing to fear at the cross?
6. What is the significance of the blood and water that flowed from the side of Christ during his crucifixion?
7. Is your conscious life more like the neck of a bottle or an open glass? Which would you like it to be?

Chapter 11

1. What are some ways you keep "Grace" waiting on the line?
2. Why does grace always catch us by surprise?
3. Why do we always seem to resist such a wonderful gift as the grace of God?
4. What is the "messy" part of grace?
5. What happens to sin and judgment when you focus on God's grace?

Chapter 12

1. Do you have any complaints to lodge with God? What should you do with those complaints?

2. How do you try to justify yourself when you blow it?
3. What grieves you about your sin?
4. How have you been a "brute beast" lately before the Lord?
5. What can you and God agree on?

Chapter 13

1. What are some ways in which culture has affected the church?
2. How has it affected you?
3. Is there ever anything wrong with being contemporary?
4. Is there ever anything wrong with being traditional?
5. How often does the cross come up in your church or form of worship?
6. What role does (should) confession play in your worship?
7. How has worship become an end in itself?
8. What's so important about the Lord's Supper (Communion)?
9. How does the cross in our lives relate to our witness to unbelievers?

Chapter 14

1. What's rugged about the cross?
2. What do you cherish about the cross?
3. How can you comprehend something less and yet love it more?
4. Have you hugged the cross today?

Chapter 15

1. Do we want to get back to the Garden as a human race?
2. What was so bad about Satan's prediction that we would know good and evil?
3. What are some examples of "good" unbelievers have done?
4. Is our redemption for us or for God?
5. What of your knowledge and/or your experience gained in reading this book are you taking away with you?

PraiseGathering Publications presents...

AN EASTER MUSICAL
WORSHIP EXPERIENCE

ON A HILL

too far away

CREATED BY

RANDY VADER
JAY ROUSE
CAMP KIRKLAND

NSPIRED BY THE BOOK **ON A HILL TOO FAR AWAY** BY JOHN FISCHER

For more information contact
PraiseGathering Music Group at 765-640-4428.

Thank you for selecting a book from
BETHANY HOUSE PUBLISHERS

Bethany House Publishers is a ministry of Bethany Fellowship International, an interdenominational, nonprofit organization committed to spreading the Good News of Jesus Christ around the world through evangelism, church planting, literature distribution, and care for those in need. Missionary training is offered through Bethany College of Missions.

Bethany Fellowship International is a member of the National Association of Evangelicals and subscribes to its statement of faith. If you would like further information, please contact:

Bethany Fellowship International
6820 Auto Club Road
Minneapolis, MN 55438 USA